by Fred DeRuvo

www.studygrowknow.com

Copyright © 2009 by Study-Grow-Know

All rights reserved. Written permission must be secured from the publisher to use or reproduce any part of this book, except brief quotations in critical reviews or articles.

Published in Scotts Valley, California, by Study-Grow-Know
www.studygrowknow.com • www.rightly-dividing.com

Scripture quotations are from The Holy Bible, English Standard Version®, copyright © 2001 by Crossway Bibles, a publishing ministry of Good News Publishers. Used by permission. All rights reserved.

Images used in this publication (unless otherwise noted) are from clipartconnection.com and used with permission, ©2007 JUPITERIMAGES, and its licensors. All rights reserved.

All Woodcuts used herein are in the Public Domain and free of copyright.

All Figure illustrations used in this book were created by the author and protected under copyright laws, © 2009.

Cover design by Fred DeRuvo

Library of Congress Cataloging-in-Publication Data

DeRuvo, Fred, 1957 –

ISBN 1442163674
EAN-13 9781442163676

1. Religion – Christian Theology - Soteriology

Contents

Chapter 1: God's Building Plan 5
Chapter 2: Accused and Convicted 66
Chapter 3: Progressively Revealed 102
Chapter 4: Multi-Faceted 117
Chapter 5: God's Overarching Purpose 144
Chapter 6: Failure is Not God's Option! 155
Chapter 7: Grace Without Human Effort 188
Chapter 8: Espousing Fear? 201
Chapter 9: Fră-Gee-Lāy 214
Chapter 10: God's Unchallenged Sovereignty 219
Resources for Your Library 224

ILLUSTRATIONS:
Figure 1: The Multi-Faceted Building Plan 8
Figure 2: God's Multi-Faceted Building Plan 9
Figure 3: Covenant Theology vs. Dispensationalism Pt 1 93
Figure 4: Covenant Theology vs. Dispensationalism Pt 2 94
Figure 5: The Parents' Plan 106
Figure 6: God's Multi-Faceted Plan 123
Figure 7: All for God's Glory 150
Figure 8: All Facets of God's Plan 152
Figure 9: Olive Tree Graphic Chart 169
Figure 10: Grace & Righteousness 186
Figure 11: Your Jobs Throughout Life 196
Figure 12: Job Blessings of Your Jobs 197
Figure 13: Rapture and the Second Coming 206
Figure 14: 1 Thessalonians 4 & Matthew 24 207
Figure 15: Premillennialism in the Old Testament 208

To those who wish to know (and are able to hear) the truth about Dispensationalism and what it actually teaches (as opposed to what it purportedly teaches), this book is dedicated.

"Salvation is an immediate display of the power of God within the lifetime and experience of the individual, and is easily distinguished from those potential accomplishments finished nearly two thousand years ago in the cross. As has been stated, salvation is a work of God for man, rather than a work of man for God. No aspect of salvation, according to the Bible, is made to depend, even in the slightest degree, on human merit or works"

(From the book, *Salvation: God's Marvelous Work of Grace*, by Lewis Sperry Chafer. Originally published in 1917, page 45).

Chapter 1
God's Building Plan

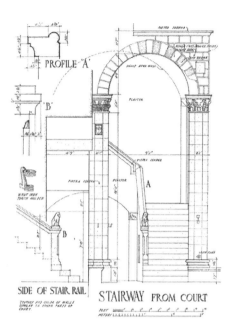

Anyone who sits down with a Bible, and begins reading from Genesis 1 onward, should have little difficulty seeing that God has revealed things to humanity *progressively*. This is difficult to argue against. When we speak of God progressively revealing His will, or plan to (and for) humanity, we mean exactly that: *"God progressively revealed His will, or plan to humanity."* It cannot be made clearer. He provided details of His plans and purposes on a need to know basis.

Please note that absolutely nothing has been stated about *salvation*. However, when discussing God's plans and purposes, it is automatically assumed by some, that salvation is the main subject. Because of that, the above statement might actually be *heard* this way: *"God progressively revealed His will, **or plan of salvation**, to humanity,"* however this is not at all what was stated.

We are *not* talking about salvation now. We are speaking about God's *purposes* and while His purposes without equivocation *include* salvation, there are many other aspects to His plans and purposes.

For instance, in his letter to the Galatians, Paul discusses the fruit of the Spirit (cf. Galatians 5:22-25). This fruit is not necessary to *receive* salvation; however, it is something that should at least *start* to become evident in each Christian's life at some point *after* salvation has been received. Alan Redpath comments, *"The ninefold cluster produces fruit in three relationships: Our relationship to God – love, joy, peace; our relationship to others – patience, kindness, goodness; our relationship to ourselves – self-control."*[1]

Once we receive salvation, the indwelling Holy Spirit begins His work within us to create the fruit that Paul speaks of in Galatians. This fruit though, is a *result* of salvation, not a prerequisite *for* it. It flows from salvation.

Another example might be that in all we do, we should live *for* Christ. Paul outlines this for us in Philippians 2:5-11 when he states, *"Have this mind among yourselves, which is yours in Christ Jesus, who, though he was in the form of God, did not count equality with God a thing to be grasped, but made himself nothing, taking the form of a servant, being born in the likeness of men. And being found in human form, he humbled himself by becoming obedient to the point of death, even death on a cross. Therefore God has highly exalted him and bestowed on him the name that is above every name, so that at the name of Jesus every knee should bow, in heaven and on earth and under the*

---

[1] Alan Redpath *The Life of Victory Devotional* (Great Britain: Christian Focus Publications 2000), June 16th date

earth, and every tongue confess that Jesus Christ is Lord, to the glory of God the Father."

While it can be argued that this mindset really only comes *after* receiving salvation, it is still something in which each Christian should cooperate with the Holy Spirit. Paul encourages us to have that same attitude that Jesus had when He walked this earth physically. This is the attitude Jesus evidenced in which He understood that all of the Father's will for Him was something to be diligently obeyed, with thankfulness.

These two areas should be mirrored in the life of every Christian because this is what God wants to see in all of His children. So while salvation is obviously a very important aspect of the entirety of God's will for us, salvation does not incorporate all of His plans and purposes. His purposes are seen in other areas, two of which have just been shown. It is the same with those particular periods in man's history, which are often referred to as *dispensations*, when God has revealed something *more* regarding the specifics of His will for that time and for those people.

To the Dispensationalist then, these unique *dispensations, stewardships,* or *ages*, have something new or unique that the previous age did not have incorporated within it. Still, this has *nothing* to do with salvation at all. It is about God *progressively* revealing His will to humanity because that is what He chose to do.

Permit Me to Build
Speaking in terms of God's progressive revelation is not unlike many things that take place in life. Maybe a good example would be the construction of a building. We know of course, that buildings do not simply plop down on the ground fully made. They are built in various sections, and in many stages. Refer to **figures 1** and **2**.

⭐ 1 The Multi-Faceted Building Plan

It takes a lot of manpower, materials and know-how to build a skyscraper

Foreman w/blueprints

Heavy Equipment

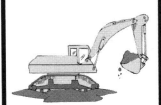
Lots of Cement!

Steel and Welders

Pipes and Fitters

Framed and Ready

Lots of Electrical Wiring

Framers

Paint and Painters

Bricks and Bricklayers

Finished Building!

✡ 2 God's Multi-Faceted Building Plan

It takes a lot of individuals and the power of the Holy Spirit to complete God's plans

 God with Word and Plans	 Adam and Eve	 Abraham and Isaac
 Moses	 Prophets for Israel	 David and Goliah
 Mary and Joseph	 Jesus and John the Baptist	**God's Fulfilled Plans!** 
 Jesus on the Cross	 Holy Spirit and the Church	*"you are...built on the foundation of the apostles and prophets, Christ Jesus himself being the cornerstone, in whom the whole structure, being joined together, grows into a holy temple in the Lord."* Eph. 2:20-22

The workers report to the construction site each day and begin working. They might be finishing the section that they were working on yesterday, or maybe they are beginning a completely new section. They work on one section at a time until the job is done.

Of course, this example is imperfect, but it serves to make the point. Someone might argue that the Engineers and Foreman have the entire plan for the project in front of them, and they *may* even show it to the workers, but it is not necessary. The workers will be able to look at the section that they are working on.

For our purposes, we will say that God is the Engineer *and* Foreman and He has chosen to keep certain aspects of His project close to His chest, so to speak, rarely showing the entire project's outcome to the workers. He is under no obligation to reveal the entire project at once.

The project starts out looking like a hole in the ground, but ends up looking like the original architectural drawings. The building goes up bit-by-bit, piece by piece, taking shape. It was always intended to *be* that building shown on the plans. It did not start out as a backyard shed and then turn into a high-rise office building when someone changed his mind. God never changed His mind.

The blueprints for this building are *many*. One sheet does not detail the entire building. There are many, many blueprints for each specific area of the building. These individual blueprints, far from competing with one another, or changing the overall project, work in perfect harmony to create the one massive structure. Each set of blueprints for specific areas does *not* represent the entire, completely finished building, but merely a part of it.

In any given building – a church, for instance – there are many aspects. Concrete creates the foundation, plumbing pipes carry the water, electrical lines direct the flow of electricity, wood, steel or aluminum is utilized for the interior skeleton, plaster or brick creates the building's exterior, insulation is used in order to make the building energy efficient, and numerous other materials are included help the building pass all of the individual code inspections. All of this is merely the structure itself. We have not even dealt with the furnishings, or many of the interior aspects.

Once all the structural work is done, the interior walls can go up, also according to the architectural blueprints. These will create the classrooms, the offices, the bathrooms, the storage closets, the kitchen and of course the sanctuary. All of these individual parts and areas together make the completed building.

No one would say that the entire finished building of a church is the sanctuary. No one would indicate that the baptistery is the completed building. These areas are *part* of the entire structure, which make up the whole of the church building. The finished building shows off the work of the original architect.

It is the same with God's plans and purposes. His plan is *not* singular, but is *multi-faceted*, yet all of those individual facets fully complement one another, working together to create the entire "edifice." Paul refers to this (cf. Ephesians 2:22), and the fact that the plans and purposes of God glorify Him mightily!

God, the Builder
Since God has chosen to reveal His plan, or will, *progressively*, it is obvious that He *knows* what it will be when it is completed because He has designed it - every part of it. Beyond this, He oversees and directs the building. It did not start out as one thing, only to switch gears and become something else entirely. The finished product will always be what it was originally *intended* to be; nothing more and nothing less. It will all be to God's glory.

Paul speaks of this in relation to the Church. He says that there are many parts, but all fit together for God's glory (cf. 1 Corinthians 12:12; Romans 12:5).

God chooses to do things for any number of reasons. By far though, there is at least one purpose, which exceeds even salvation, as hard as that may be to believe, and it is this: **everything God does is for His glory**. That is important enough to repeat. *Everything God does is for His glory.*

In eternity past, in the council of the Godhead, everything was all mapped out *at that time* regarding the events which would occur in this universe and on this planet, from start to finish. He either caused directly, or allowed all events to occur. God's absolute and ultimate purpose is that *all* of His creation will see His revealed purposes (plural) and *all* of those purposes will ultimately give Him glory. They will do so by coming under the banner of His full sovereignty.

Everything that God does or allows can be summed up in that one purpose: *for His glory*. There can be no denial of that. We will look into that in more detail as we move through the pages of this book, so hang on.

All Those Trees!
One more example before we move on. You are hiking along, enjoying the beauty of another day that the Lord has made. It is peaceful, as the warmth of the sun shines down on you, and you hear the birds as they sing. The smells of nature fill the air. You have been following a small stream to your right since you started out on your hike. It has always been there, moving steadily along with you as you walk. The open air is just what you needed to relax and refresh you after a week of stress at work.

You continue moving along the trail, and up ahead you see the entrance to a forest. You knew from your maps that it was there, so you continue walking and before you know it, you have entered under the canopy of large redwoods. It is striking! The air still smells wonderful, but of course now has a distinctly pine flavor to it. The sun no longer beats down directly on you, but you can still see its rays filtering through the branches in the trees above.

As you move along, the forest becomes thicker with trees and you find that it is now becoming darker since the tops of the trees block out more of your view. You are not worried though, because you know it is still early in the afternoon; plenty of time for you to continue your hike, stop for some lunch and then head back to your car.

The stream you have been following is still present and in fact, has gotten bigger. Eventually you hear the sound of a powerful current up ahead and you perk up. You move a bit more quickly and the sound of the water continues to grow louder. Soon you see it, and there you decide to rest on the bank overlooking the fast moving current. Above you, off to the left is a waterfall. The mist from it sprays lightly over your face. Ah. This is even more relaxing than the walk through the field!

You decide to have your lunch here, and then when finished, you begin again to move out. You complete your trail a few hours later, which incidentally winds all the way around back to your car. After a few more wistful looks at the surrounding scenery, you head back to town and your home, refreshed and ready for another week.

The point here is that the forest never changed, did it? It was the exact same forest whether you were in the field *before* you entered the forest, as you entered it, as you came to the middle of it, or as you exited that same forest. *Nothing* about the forest changed. What changed was your *position* in the forest, which allowed you to hear and see *new* things all around you. When you first entered, you saw and smelled the trees. The sun above you was still warm and visible. As you moved further into the forest, the trees became closer together and the sun was more difficult to see. The sun itself was the same as before you entered the forest. It had not changed.

You continued and eventually came to the waterfall. Had it been there the whole time? Of course, but you simply had not noticed it because you were not close enough to hear or see it yet. As far as you knew, there was merely a small stream meandering its way through the forest.

Please remember, this narrative is an imperfect analogy, only used to emphasize a point. Do not make the mistake of thinking too hard about it. For instance, just because I stated that the stream grew in size, I am *not* implying (or surreptitiously stating), that it represents salvation, and therefore salvation has *changed*. Salvation has never changed. Just look at it as a basic analogy; nothing more and nothing less. There is certainly nothing allegorical in the narrative.

In the end, the only thing that changed was your position as you moved across the field and into the forest. This allowed you to see more of the forest and all that was included within it. Had you remained on the outside of the woods, never venturing inside, you would not have seen or heard the waterfall that was always there. You would not have smelled the pine, or seen that the trees which grew close together, blocking out light from the sun. Nothing about the forest changed. What changed was *you*. Your perspective or point of view changed.

It is the same with God's revelation. It is progressively revealed through His Word. This however, does *not* mean that because it is revealed bit by bit, that the overarching plan of God somehow *changes*. It does *not at all* change. God's plans for humanity were determined before the creation of anything, and they were decided in eternity past within the council of the Godhead. What we experience or live through is simply God's *unfolding*, or progressively revealed will for us.

In the Beginning

So what does all of this have to do with God's progressive will, if it is not discussing salvation? It has everything to do with it. It allows us to see in a tangible way that in our physical world, *all of His will* works together to form one complete whole, and all parts support the sum total. It also provides us with the overall purpose for all of the plans that God has created which He has married into one huge plan. Like the many spokes of a wheel all of them joining at the center, so is God's multi-faceted will.

Just because we do not see the entire building all at once, or are unable to view the entire forest together, does not mean that it was not there to begin with as it had been created. God does things His way and He has chosen to reveal aspects of His will piece by piece; but the end, or the culmination of all of those facets meet where they are supposed to meet.

I remember years ago visiting New York City. As we walked through Manhattan, we came close to the Empire State Building. When we got right underneath it, just across the street from it, I looked up. It was not possible to see the top because as it went up, the building got narrower. The wider floors below kept the top of the building out of sight. The top was still there though, but from that vantage point, I was unable to see it.

Turn to Genesis chapter one. It is here that we become privy to some of the aspects of the Most High's will with respect to His Creation. On each of six days, He created different things, according to His plan, will, and purposes. We also know that on the seventh day, He rested. Everything He had created He declared to be "good."

After their creation, Adam and Eve walked and worked in the Garden of Eden and had only one major responsibility in the form of a negative: to avoid eating the fruit of the Tree of Knowledge of Good and Evil. That was it. That was the one *rule* that God gave them. It was the first of His many progressive revelations to humanity. "Do not eat of that tree." God *began* the process of revealing His moral code, and revelation of it came from *His spoken Word*. There were no other rules that we know of at that point in time. The only other *responsibilities* then were to tend the garden, care for the earth, and have dominion over all other creatures.

Innocence to Believe
During this trial period, Adam and Eve were what we would call *innocent*. They had not yet sinned and because of that had no *experiential* knowledge of sin at all. Experiential knowledge of sin would not have created an undue burden on them, had they gotten that knowledge directly from God *without* sinning. They instead chose to circumvent God altogether and go by what the Serpent said. This certainly gave them access to that experiential knowledge of sin but they got it the wrong way: by *actually* sinning, as we know.

All that Adam and Eve *were required* to do was to remember God's one rule and to <u>*believe*</u> Him when He said that if they broke that rule, they would die. *Believing* God was the most important thing that either of them could do at that point (and interestingly enough, it is the most important thing anyone can do *today*). To disbelieve God was tantamount *to,* and a precursor *of* what ultimately became their *action* of disobedience. Had they continued to believe God, not switching allegiance to the Tempter, the action stemming from that continued belief would have been obedience, resulting in *righteousness*.

Prior to the fall, it was *belief* that promoted obedience with a proper attitude. *Believing* God provides the necessary confidence, along with a correct attitude and even a love of and appreciation for the recipient of the belief: in this case, God. All of this together prompts the correct *action*.

One day the Tempter came along and the first thing he did was to get Adam and Eve to *question* God's *credibility*. Put another way, he planted the strong seed of *doubt*. Consequently, after giving the Tempter an ear, they wound up agreeing with him, which of course caused *doubt* to replace *belief* in God's Word. Satan called God a liar and they wound up agreeing. Notice please, that God was conspicuously not visibly present (though He *was* there). Once Adam and Eve agreed that God was lying, it was fairly easy to take that step of disobedience, which caused the entire Creation to be cursed.

Since they were innocent of the knowledge that the fruit of the Tree of Good and Evil would produce within them, Dispensationalists refer to this period of time before the Fall (however brief or long it was) as the Age (or Dispensation) of Innocence. The reason we do so is because as soon as Adam and Eve sinned, things changed and *they* changed drastically. Innocence was gone. Nothing remained the same, except God Himself and His plans.

In the place of innocence, there existed a cold, hard, face-to-face with impending doom and death. This, in turn, grew into the accompanying physical discomfort that aging and death bring.

Working for Salvation?
Many Covenant Theologians refer to this period prior to the fall as the Covenant of *Works*. "*The covenant of works was contingent on the uncertain obedience of a changeable man, while the covenant of grace rests on the obedience of Christ as Mediator, which is absolute and certain.*"[2] It is believed that there was a *covenant* made between God and Adam, and it was based on *obedience*. Had Adam been *obedient*, they say, he would have then gained eternal life.

---

[2] Louis Berkhof *Systematic Theology* (Grand Rapids: Eerdmans 1996), 272

Unfortunately, the Covenant Theologian at this point believes salvation would have been offered to Adam and Eve based solely on their ability to *obey* God. Salvation then, for the Covenant Theologian who espouses this view, was based on *works*. This is even more confusing when it is clear from their own testimony that they *accuse* Dispensationalism of advocating two-methods of salvation: one of grace and works and one of grace only. Does not their belief that this initial part of man's existence was governed by *works* state that salvation was *merited* not by God's favor, but by what man *did*? However, we certainly want to give them the benefit of the doubt related to their position, so let's continue on to see what we uncover.

As I have shown, the disobedience was merely symptomatic of the underlying problem in Adam and Eve; the outcome of choosing to *stop* believing in God's Word. The ability to obey or not, begins *within* each person. Satan knew this, and this is precisely *why* he chose to approach Eve to tempt her to reconsider God's character. He knew if he could get her to *begin* to question God's believability, the resultant disobedience would be a foregone conclusion; merely a step away. Therefore, it happened, just as Satan hoped (and as God allowed).

Eve was tempted to question part of God's *character*. She considered it, and then thought, *"Hmmm, the Serpent makes a good point. The fruit is good to look at! I bet the Serpent is right! I bet God doesn't want us to be like He is! Well, that's not fair!"*

This line of reasoning quickly escalated into a full-blown desire to eat the fruit. This we know she did. Then the text tells us that she offered it to her husband and he ate as well.

I am not at all sure what was going on in Adam's head. The text gives us no indication of what he was doing, or even if he was present. I used to think that Adam was off somewhere tending to another part of the garden and that the Serpent took on Eve while she was apart from her husband. It was my thinking that the Serpent would have found it easier to approach Eve when she was by herself, with Adam off doing something else. Because of this, I envisioned Eve giving in to the temptation to eat of the fruit and *then* going to find her husband and giving it to him.

I really do not know what to think, frankly. The text could be taken that way, but it is probably best to understand that Adam had been standing right there listening to the entire conversation and watching his wife eat of the fruit.

In either case, we see that Adam put up no struggle whatsoever; no disagreement. He had probably already made his own decision about the forbidden fruit. Paul tells us that Adam was not deceived like Eve (cf. 1 Timothy 2:14). He sinned deliberately, according to the Scriptures.

Had Adam been away from Eve, maybe, after she found him, their conversation would have gone something like this:

"Honey?" calls Eve.

"Yes, dear?" responds Adam.

"Here is the fruit from that ol' tree which sits in the middle of the garden; the one we're not supposed to eat," says Eve.

"What about it?" asks Adam

"Isn't it pretty? Smells good, too," says Eve.

"Yes. Looks really juicy," states Adam.

"Take a bite. I did. It's really good," exclaims Eve.

Adam takes a bite. The rest becomes human history.

In yet another scenario, the situation might have unfolded something like this:

The two of them are standing around not far from the tree that they are supposed to avoid, when Satan, in the form of the Serpent, slithers on up...

"Morning. How are you folks doing today?" asks the Serpent.

"Fine, thank you," responds Eve.

Adam simply looks and nods slightly.

"Nice garden, isn't it?" asks Satan, merely appearing just to make small talk.

"Beautiful! I cannot believe that we have this all to ourselves!" cries Eve with joy.

All three of them take a moment or two to drink in the surroundings, marveling at the beauty that God had created.

"So, I hear it's your job to tend the garden and keep everything beautiful," continues the Serpent, looking at Eve.

"Yes, that's Adam's job," the exulted Eve smiles. "Adam is supposed to take care of the plants and animals and make sure that everything gets what it needs."

"I see," says the Serpent. "Sounds like a big job."

"Yes, but as you can see, we have plenty of food to eat," replies Eve. "The Lord God made certain that we would have everything to meet our needs."

The Serpent nods his head in agreement, smiling slightly as he looks around. He glances at Adam, smiles, and then turns back to Eve, smiling to her as well. He then looks a bit past both of them and up.

"Say now, *there's* a beautiful tree!" exclaims the Serpent. "I bet the fruit from that one tastes really good!"

Adam looks over at the tree and his smile fades. Eve also looks over, and a more serious look overtakes her face.

"Oh, that one. We have not eaten of that fruit yet," says Eve.

"Really?!" exclaims the Serpent in mock surprise. "Wow, that's too bad because as good as every fruit in this garden looks, *that* fruit looks as if it would taste the best! I'm just curious, but why have you not tasted it yet? Are you two kids waiting for some special occasion?"

Adam starts to speak, but is interrupted by Eve, so he simply waits and smiles, allowing her to finish.

"Oh, we're not supposed to eat or even touch that tree! It's completely off limits. If we did, we would die. God told Adam, and Adam told me, so I know it's true," says Eve.

The Big "Are You Sure?"
"What?!" responds Satan incredulously. "You *can't* be serious! Don't you think that's a bit drastic? You don't really think you would actually die, do you?"

Moving in a bit closer, and lowering his voice a bit, the Serpent continues, "I bet God simply doesn't want you to be like Him: knowing the difference between good and evil. That's probably what would happen if you ate that fruit."

All three remain quiet and stare at the Tree of Knowledge of Good and Evil.

"Yep, what a beautiful tree," says Satan quietly, to no one in particular.

Eve looks over at Adam and Adam looks at Eve. She inches forward toward the tree. Glancing over at Adam, who says and does nothing, Eve continues the few remaining steps to the tree.

"You know Adam, this fruit really *does* look wonderful for food!" exclaims Eve. "It smells so beautiful too!"

Adam continues looking at Eve, to see what she will do.

"I bet the Serpent's right. I bet eating it *would* make us wise!" insists Eve. She takes the fruit, brings it to her mouth and eats.

Adam – still the big, silent type – waits and says nothing. As Eve bites into the fruit, Adam smells its sweet aroma from where he stands.

"Surely God did not mean what He said to me," thinks Adam. "I must have misunderstood. After all, I'm supposed to rule the entire earth! How can I rule the *whole* earth if there is part of it that I don't have control over?!"

Eve reaches out toward Adam, handing him the fruit. Adam puts out his hand and takes the fruit. He considers the fruit ever so briefly, then, after looking at Eve, he eats of it as well.

Once they have both eaten, they look at themselves and see their nakedness for the first time. Man, is *that* embarrassing! In fact, it was so embarrassing that they run to make coverings from large leaves!

Well, we know the rest of the story.

It *Started* with Unbelief and *Ended* with Disobedience

The question is, where did their sin *start*? Did it actually *start* when Eve *ate* the fruit? No, it did not *start* with disobedience. It *ended* with disobedience!

James commented on this when he wrote to other Jews who had been dispersed, "*each person is tempted when he is lured and enticed by his own desire. Then desire when it has conceived gives birth to sin, and sin when it is fully grown brings forth death*" (James 1:14-15).

The sin began in their inner *desires*. It was fanned into a flame because they *agreed* with the Tempter that God had lied to them. Once they agreed with him on it, it was a very short step over the line to allowing their sinful desires to become a physical act.

The entire internal process may have taken a very short time, or may have occurred little by little over a few days or more, culminating in the brief conversation with the Serpent. They may have looked at the tree at times, and maybe even *thought* about how the fruit might have tasted. They may even have had *conversations* about what the fruit might have tasted like, based on its smell, which was undoubtedly carried on the breeze throughout the Garden at times.

It may also be that Satan was privy to their conversations about the tree, or maybe it is possible that he was able to tempt them with their thoughts, or somehow direct their attention to the tree. In other words, he could have softened them up over a period of time (however long that might have been) prior to sinning. When he felt they were softened up enough, he went in for the kill, by dropping the big bomb on them, which got them to question God's truthfulness.

Who knows exactly what occurred up to the point where Satan took over the body of the Serpent? What we *do* know is that as James has said, Eve's sin (and then Adam's) began with *desire*. The desire grew until it took very little effort or suggestion on the part of the Serpent to help them decide just to *go for it*. James is very clear here, that our inner desires give *birth* to sin.

The reason I have taken this much space to deal with this issue is to show that the sin of disobedience *stems* from something *internal*. Whether it is desire, or questioning God's character (or in this case, both), the disobedience is merely the *result* of the internal thought process and the decision that was made *there*, within the heart. In effect, if this is true, they had already sinned within themselves before they actually ate. The disobedience of actually eating the fruit merely outwardly fulfilled the unbelief and disobedience they already felt *inwardly*.

The Outward Manifestation of the Inner Reality
What we see throughout the Bible over and over again is the truth that disobedience, or rebellion (which is the same thing), is the *outward manifestation* of the *inner reality*. First, there are suggestions either by our own thoughts, or by some outside stimulus. If we give heed to this stimulus, it will give rise to *unbelief* inwardly. Once we have reached that point, the outward manifestation of what is internal occurs naturally.

Covenant?
In reviewing the situation with God and His command to Adam, there seems to be absolutely no covenant of works in view, where Adam and Eve were concerned. What they went through was a test to determine what Adam and Eve would do with true, unadulterated *freedom of choice*; something we do not experience as *they* experienced (and this is precisely why God remained invisible in the situation, so as not to influence their decision one way or another). Had God been visibly with them at that time, the outcome would have been different. At the same time, I certainly cannot imagine the Tempter even striking up the conversation with Eve had God been visibly present.

Adam and Eve's *salvation* was not based on what they *did*. It was based on what they *believed*. Sin began there and the external demonstration of that internal sin became evident. The question was "Who would they believe: God or Satan?"

Inner Lust Can Lead to Outward Acts
We know that a man who lusts after a woman and then enters into an illicit relationship with her is guilty of sin. However, we also know from Jesus that a man who lusts in his heart after a woman, but does *not* go beyond that into the actual physical act of adultery, is also guilty of sin (cf. Matthew 5:28). According to Jesus, there is *no* differ-

ence, as far as God is concerned, between these two situations. *Both* result in sin. God sees *both* circumstances, and He sees the *intentions of the heart* in both circumstances, which, as we have readily seen, is where sin begins.

The only saving grace (if you can call it that) is that when a man lusts in his heart but *goes no further*, he has only sinned against God, which is certainly bad enough, but he has *not* ruined his or other people's lives by actually entering into a physical relationship with the woman of his lustful thoughts. When a man lusts and takes it to its unfortunate natural conclusion by having a real affair, he has still sinned against God. Now he has *also* sinned against his wife (if he is married), the other woman's husband (if she is married), and quite possibly other people as well.

David Vividly Sins

In 1 Samuel 11, we learn that King David lusted for Bathsheba, who happened to be bathing herself at the time. Had he stopped there, and literally *run* from that sin, imagine what would *not* have occurred! He would have confessed his sin before God and would have been restored with no consequences existing *outside* of him, except for the possibility that he should have been with his own troops as they fought a war, instead of hanging out at home. Had he been with his troops that alone would have kept the situation with Bathsheba from happening, along with the tragedies that followed. But that aside, we know what *did* take place. We know that King David 1) lusted after Bathsheba, and then 2) *allowed that sin to give birth to the physical act of adultery.* Of course, he immediately felt guilty, but instead of confessing his sin, he 3) tried to cover it, first by 4) tricking Bathsheba's husband Uriah, into sleeping with her before the next battle. When that did not work, David 5) chose to have Uriah killed during battle. The entire situation wound up going from bad to worse.

Is This the Same David?
It is so difficult to believe that this same David who had slain Goliath and lived a life of reverence toward God, came to a point of deciding that murdering someone was the only way to cover his own sin. So, Uriah the Hittite was killed in battle *deliberately* because David's orders were that the other men surrounding Uriah should pull back, allowing him to be overcome by enemy forces.

Of course, God was not blind to any of this, but David was beyond the ability to hear God by then. While he continued to have his salvation, he was certainly out of fellowship with God, to say the least. God chose to send Nathan the prophet to tell David a story. As it turns out, the story was about David himself, though he did not realize that at first, so Nathan had to point that out to him.

It was with that realization that God brought the hammer down in judgment upon David. It is terribly tragic to read all that occurred because of David's physical sin, which began with a hidden inner *desire* that gave birth to *adultery* and then *murder*. That is extremely tragic, but this is one thing about the Bible that counteracts all the claims of its critics: God is *not* afraid to show the faults, foibles, and outright sin of the people He has chosen for His purposes. Such was the case with David.

What we can learn from this situation is that there is not one person who is beyond being tempted to commit sin who can wind up not only destroying his or her own life, but other people's lives as well. We are all in the same boat with a fallen nature. We sin because we have it, and it helps Satan achieve his ends. Fortunately, for those of us who are in a real relationship with Christ, His forgiveness extends to us and our fellowship can be renewed with Him once we confess our sin to Him. In fact, the Bible tells us *"If we confess our sins, he is faithful and just to forgive us our sins and to cleanse us from all unrighteousness"* (1 John 1:9). Please notice that we are not told we need to ask for forgiveness. That was already accomplished when we received Christ as Savior and Lord. Our responsibility as Christians is to confess any sin that we know of, or that the Holy Spirit brings to our attention. A sincere confession to Him allows us to keep a short record and quickly get back into fellowship with Him.

Not long ago, I had gotten into a situation where I was simply not a good steward of some money that my wife and I had. I went ahead without praying, without thinking, and used it. When we got into a bind because of it, my first impulse was to be angry. How could God let us get into this bind? I felt self-confident, but I am forever grateful that in spite of my blustering, He reminded me that I was the one who had spent the money and I had done so without thinking or praying. Upon realizing this, I felt terrible. I could do nothing but agree with God and for the next few minutes all I could say to Him was *"Lord, I am SO sorry. I know you forgive me, but I am so terribly sorry for doing what I did. I know that you are not required by any stretch to help us here, in light of the fact that I acted foolishly. For that, I am really very sorry. I am so sorry for my stupidity. Would you be kind to us, in spite of my stupidity and provide us with a way out of this?"*

God had no obligation to help me. I felt terrible, but let me stress that what I was *not* feeling was *guilt*. There was a bit of guilt when I was speaking out of my own self-confidence, but as soon as God, through the Holy Spirit, helped me understand that I was wrong, I *confessed*. As bad as I felt during the confession of my sin to God, I felt *no* guilt whatsoever. I knew He loved me; however, I did not know what He might do to help me. I can say that He honored my confession and helped us through that situation. It is interesting, as I look back, to see how that situation has helped me to become more willing to wait for Him and His leading. I now take things to Him more regularly and when I am not sure what I should do, I have learned to continue to pray and wait.

God's love for David never stopped, but His anger burned toward him, just as a loving father might become angry with a wayward child who had made some asinine decision in life. Of course, the truth is that the sins, which David committed, were not what we might term "little." They were big, causing a great deal of harm and injustice. It becomes clear that God's level of anger is commensurate with the degree of David's sin. All sin breaks God's law and John tells us that all sin is lawlessness (cf. 1 John 3:4). We cannot think that we are better off because we have only committed "small" or "light" sins. We may only better off as far as *societal* consequences are concerned. As far as God is concerned, sin is sin and it all needs to be punished.

Adam and Eve
Though they sinned, God did not stop loving Adam and Eve. While He was angry that they had given in to the temptation to think that God was a liar, He did not give up on them. In fact, it seems clear from Scripture that this whole situation was designed by God to point to the number one reason why God does anything. In Genesis 3, we see that the built in redeeming feature of God's pronouncement of judgment was that ultimately, humankind would have a Savior and from that Savior, would come the offer of redemption to humanity. Adam and Eve's failure to obey did not take God by surprise. He was fully prepared for it and *knew* that they would choose to be disobedient.

However, the truth is that their salvation was not based on *works* here. It was based solely on faith, just as our salvation is today. It is unfortunate that there are many people who have been fooled into thinking that these two were under an actual covenant from which they had to *earn* their salvation. No such situation existed. All they were required to do was to avoid the fruit of that particular tree. Had they continued believing God's Word, this would not have been a problem.

By way of example, the physical act of adultery cannot occur without an initial and deliberate lusting. It is lust that we toy with, enjoy, and tempt ourselves. We spend time enlarging upon it, and dwelling on it, and all of this brings us closer and closer to the *physical* act of committing adultery. Without the desire within, how could the actual physical act come to fruition?

There is only one way to fight lust, as with all sin. Instead of giving *in* to the temptation to lust, each individual should deliberately move away from it. The temptation, which begins in his mind should be replaced with prayer, Scripture, or even purposefully redirecting the thinking to something else entirely. In doing so, the individual being tempted *believes* and *agrees* with God that lust is *sin* and sin is lawlessness. Believing God's stated Word results in obedience. Obedience glorifies God. The result for the Christian is greater maturity, wisdom, and spiritual growth.

It is no different *now* from during Adam and Eve's situation. They were not under any kind of covenant or arrangement of *works*. They were under *grace*, and their choice was simply to *believe* God or not. The corresponding action would naturally flow from that. This is how it is with us as well.

When we are tempted to lust (or to commit any sin), we have two choices: 1) to give in to it, or 2) resist that temptation (cf. James 4:7). Satan is the source of much temptation and he usually knows where to hit us because he sees the chinks in our "armor." He sees us when we are alone, and not interacting with others. He tends to know what we do in private and of course, he uses that to his advantage. If he does not personally involve himself in knowing, he has an entire network of fallen angels at his disposal continually who do his dirty work.

By resisting temptation, we are resisting the attempted work of the devil, in whatever form that temptation comes to us. This same idea was at work when Christ was tempted in the wilderness (cf. Mark 1:12-13). With each temptation that Satan threw at our Lord, Jesus responded with Scripture and resisted Satan's attempts to get Him to sin. Eventually, Christ simply said "away with you!" to Satan and Satan left. He will not leave forever, that is certain, but we should put up the same resistance each time.

Realistically, we are not able to live without sinning in this life. We will, at times give in to the temptation to sin. Sometimes, the act of sin occurs so swiftly that it seems to happen without thinking of it. If someone is prone to having a temper, chances are good that it will take little impetus for their anger to come to the surface. It will seem as if that person did not even *get* the chance to resist. This is because of the pattern that has built up over the years, and that pattern needs to be *unlearned*. Studying the Word and staying close to the Lord through fellowship with Him, will accomplish this, over time.

Getting back to Adam and Eve, a good question to ask about that situation is whether God had told them the truth about the forbidden fruit. That was the *only* question that they needed to answer. Should they continue to believe God, or switch allegiances by believing the Tempter, thereby accusing God of lying? They chose to side with the Tempter and in doing so, chose to *stop* believing God. As stated, the action, which resulted from that decision, simply proved what existed within them.

What is This Conscience?
Because of the tragedy that resulted from believing Satan, Adam and Eve became all too aware of their own shame and guilt. They knew they failed not merely themselves, but also God. By believing the enemy of their souls, they essentially told God that He was not trustworthy.

Their shame and guilt also showed itself in the realization of their nakedness. They had not noticed their nakedness before, because there was nothing wrong with it. It was part of God's plan at that time that they should enjoy and subdue the earth and not have to worry about or deal with covering themselves. There had been no need to be covered. They did not need to worry about animals attacking them, stubbing their toe, or breaking an arm. In their present sinful condition, clothing and footwear would offer some protection against these dangers. They had become corrupted by their abject refusal to believe God's Word.

What caused this feeling of shame? Their *conscience*. Their sin had activated their conscience and they now knew that they had done wrong, because not only they knew intellectually that they had done what God told them *not* to do, but also because they *felt* that they had done wrong. This is how conscience works and this is why this period of time beginning in Genesis 4 is often referred to by Dispensationalists as The Dispensation (or Age) of Conscience.

Salvation Anyone?
We have mainly talked about salvation only *indirectly*. For the most part, we are simply discussing the different *levels of responsibility* connected with these different ages. We are discussing how God provided more accountability to humanity by supplying more information from the one age to the next. This we refer to as His *progressive revelation*. Ryrie comments, *"Covenant theology, then, because of the rigidity of its unifying principle of the covenant of grace, can never show within its system proper progress of revelation."*[3] It is clear that the Covenant theologian can point out little to no difference between the various periods that the Dispensationalist points out. Ryrie continues, *"Dispensationalism, on the other hand, can and does give proper place to the idea of development. Under the various administrations*

---

[3] Charles C. Ryrie *Dispensationalism (Revised/Expanded)* (Chicago: Moody 2007), 23

of God, different revelation was given to man, and that revelation was increasingly progressive in the scope of its content."[4]

Interestingly enough, Covenant theologians also break down Scripture into various sections, as Ryrie indicates, *"After rejecting the usual dispensational scheme of Bible distinctions, [Louis Berkhof] enumerates his own scheme of dispensations or administrations, reducing the number to two – the Old Testament dispensation and the New Testament dispensation. However, within the Old Testament dispensation, Berkhof lists four subdivisions, which, although he terms them 'stages in the revelation of the covenant of grace,' are distinguishable enough to be listed. In reality, then, he finds these four plus the New Testament dispensation, or five periods of differing administrations of God. Thus, the covenant theologian finds biblical distinctions a necessary part of his theology, even though the covenant of grace is his ruling category."*[5]

The fact is that the covenant theologian recognizes that God works differently in the various periods of biblical history. For the Dispensationalist though, these ages or periods, while initiating and highlighting different levels of responsibility, have absolutely *nothing* directly to do with salvation on any basis apart from grace, even though this is the oft-repeated charge *against* Dispensationalism.

The various dispensations simply purport to show, as Ryrie states, *"the orderly progress of revelation throughout Scripture. [The] dispensations are not stages in the revelation of the covenant of grace, but are God's distinctive and different administrations in directing the affairs of the world."*[6]

It is because of the fact that Adam's conscience came into being after the fall that the Dispensationalist has chosen to label this dispensation *The Age of Conscience.* Prior to their fall, they were innocent of

---

[4] Ibid
[5] Ibid, 20
[6] Charles C. Ryrie *Dispensationalism (Revised/Expanded)* (Chicago: Moody 2007), 20

any wrongdoing, and so the dispensation is often labeled *The Age of Innocence*.

We note that in the period immediately following the fall of Adam and Eve, God was now *adding* to the initial level of responsibility, which existed under the Dispensation of Conscience. Prior to this, there was essentially one requirement of Adam and Eve, which was not to eat of the tree, which grew the forbidden fruit. Their responsibilities however, included subduing the land and have dominion over it and the animals. These responsibilities continued from the Age of Innocence into the Age of Conscience.

What has *not* changed is God's requirement that He should always be *believed*. Humanity has always had a tough time with that. Believing is the foundational requirement for salvation as far as *man* is concerned. God has done all the hard work. Man needs merely to believe, and to believe in spite of how things may appear, or the lies that the enemy whispers in our ears. God expects to be believed because in Him there is only truth (cf. Numbers 23:19; Deuteronomy 32:4; 1 Samuel 15:29; John 14:6; 17:17; 18:37-38; Romans 3:4; 2 Thessalonians 2:10-13; Titus 1:1-2). He is incapable of lying.

Innocent No Longer
Obviously things had to change from *Innocence* to *Conscience* because Adam and Eve *themselves* had changed. Nothing could really stay the same. Not only Adam and Eve, but also the entire earth along with the animal kingdom, had seriously been altered by our first parents' agreement with the Temper. They could no longer be called Innocent because they were well *past* that stage. They now *experientially* understood the difference between good and evil. Contrary to the tone of Eden prior to the Fall, God had now placed a curse on the entire earth and everything that inhabited it, including Eden.

It was during this time – *the Age of Conscience* - that God, by the Holy Spirit, began using man's conscience to point out the approach of sin through temptation. By giving heed to temptation, and obeying its desires, sin was the result and conscience would then go back and forth, from warning of impending sin, to accusing of impending judgment, depending upon which side of sin the individual was standing.

God spoke through conscience so that man would have opportunity to follow God and *not* give in to sin. The problem was the *lack* of desire on man's part to follow God. It must be stated that since man chose to disregard God's one law under Innocence, there was even less of a chance that he would obey God under Conscience. Man had essentially turned his back on God. He now chose to follow his own dictates, which were in actuality, the Tempter's suggestion. Did this somehow take God by surprise? Of course not. God has *never* been surprised by *anything*. How could He be the all-knowing God if anything took Him by surprise?

Something would have to be provided to humanity so that when men did sin, they would not feel completely hopeless, but would begin to learn that there was a way back to God, instated by God Himself. That something was in the form of the *sacrificial system*.

Adam's Leafy Loincloth
Note that in actuality, the sacrificial system had already begun. In the Garden of Eden, Adam and Eve did their best to cover their sin. They really tried. However, not even their efforts to deal with their sin were up to God's righteous standards. Did they think God would simply not notice?

God: *Why have you covered yourself with leaves, Eve?* (As if God would not know...)

Eve: *What this?! This ol' thing?! Uh...hmmm, I...hmmm.*

In Genesis 3, we read that God came to them and, after pronouncing judgment (which included the curse), He made for them clothing of *skins*. Without the text having to actually state it, it is obvious that God *killed* animals, shedding *their* blood so that Adam and Eve could have their "shame" covered by the skin of the animals. This was the beginnings of the sacrificial system later iterated by Moses.

I remember speaking with an individual about the Fall of man and the results of it. We were discussing the clothing of skins that God provided for Adam and Eve. When I mentioned that God had killed the animals, the individual I was speaking with was floored. God would *never* kill the animals for that! He was unable to believe that, apparently preferring to believe that God made the skins simply appear. The text states *"And the LORD God made for Adam and for his wife garments of skins and clothed them,"* (Genesis 3:21). It seems clear enough that the implied meaning here is that God had to kill some animals so that He could fashion proper clothing for Adam and Eve. In so doing, blood was shed, which was the beginning of the sacrificial system, to become more refined through Moses, and perfected in Christ's atonement on Calvary's cross (cf. Hebrews 2:14-17; 4:14-15; 7:11-14, 27; 9:11-22; 10:1-39; 12:1-2).

The coverings that Adam and Eve created would in no way take care of their sin. Blood needed shedding, and while the shed blood of animals would not cancel the sin, it would temporarily *cover* it. Since the cross is always before God, He has always had a way of *passing over sin* for those who believe. Romans 3:24 states, *"[we] are justified by his grace as a gift, through the redemption that is in Christ Jesus, whom God put forward as a propitiation by his blood, to be received by faith. This was to show God's righteousness, because in his divine forbearance he had passed over former sins."*

Commenting on this, John MacArthur states, *"Now that great text tells us what the cross meant to God. What the death of Christ, the atoning work of Christ, the blood- shedding sacrifice of Christ meant to God.*

Four things stand out. It declared God's righteousness, it exalted God's grace, it revealed God's consistency and it confirmed God's Word."[7]

This entire situation must have been terribly traumatic for Adam and Eve to witness. They likely felt bad enough because of what they had done. They could no longer go back to that time when they did not know the difference between right and wrong. They were now experiencing and thinking things that heretofore had been foreign to them. They would soon begin experiencing many more things that they had not experienced either, like sweating from work or heat, stubbing a toe or breaking a bone, being angry, worrying, or feeling alone or lonely, along with everything else that results from the fallen nature and the curse on the earth.

They had also never been eyewitnesses to animal slaughter, and they themselves had not yet experienced physical death or pain before either. Now they watched in horror as an innocent animal was slain and the life that once had flowed through its veins was now flowing out onto the ground (the life of every creature is in its blood, which is why Christ had to *shed blood*: cf. Genesis 9:3-6; Leviticus 17:11; Deuteronomy 12:23).

Please note that even with this first act of sacrifice on God's part (sacrificing an *innocent* animal), their sin was merely *covered*, not eradicated or canceled. They watched as God took an animal(s) and made *it* the sacrifice for *their* sin of disbelief. Talk about heaping shame upon guilt! Watching God put an animal to death, and then skinning it must have really driven the point home to them. They could not *possibly* miss the impact of what God was teaching them, but it is also very likely that God took the time to explain things in detail during this time. Certainly, we know that Adam and Eve understood it and explained it to their sons, Cain and Abel (cf. Genesis 4:1-16).

---

[7] John MacArthur *Looking at the Cross from God's Perspective* (Sermon on Romans 3:24-31 © 1997 Grace to You)

Of course we as Christians understand that the killing of the innocent for the guilty was God's way of introducing the system that would eventually find its complete and perfect fulfillment thousands of years later in Jesus. It was the beginning of a system that ultimately pointed to one future event. That event was Jesus Christ's death on Calvary's cross. Adam and Eve were both unaware of the ultimate future outcome of what they witnessed that day. The revealing of that definitive aspect of God's plan would take place slowly, over centuries, as God *progressively* unveiled His plan of redemption to humanity.

Sin Incurs Debt That Must Be Paid
God was teaching Adam and Eve that because of *their* unbelief, which resulted in disobedience, the consequence was sin along with their immediate *spiritual,* and eventual *physical* deaths. Due to this, something terribly drastic needed to be done, if the problem was ever going to be corrected in God's righteous eyes. Blood needed to be shed. Innocent life had to be given in exchange for their sin. So not only did *they* begin the physical process of dying through aging, now animals that had absolutely *nothing* to do with their sin were required to give their life (involuntarily) in order to *provide* for them. Christ's *voluntary* death thousands of years later, would be the culminating act of God's plan of salvation.

Please remember though, the blood of those animals did *not* in any way, shape, or form *remove* the sin permanently or actually cancel the debt created by sin. It merely allowed God to pass over it by superficially covering it.

Let me quote from my old green binder from Philadelphia College of Bible. It states *"The sacrifices of the Old Testament did not 'take away sin' Heb. 10:1-4."*[8] This is exactly what I was taught when I attended PCB: that the OT sacrifices did not remove or cancel out sin. These

---

[8] Dr. Clarence E. Mason, Jr., *Soteriology* (Philadelphia: PCB 1971), 1

sacrifices did not make salvation available. The sacrifices simply *pointed* to the One who would in actuality make salvation possible.

Here is the sentence immediately following the one just quoted from that same green binder: *"The Biblical meaning of 'atonement' is nothing more than 'to cover.' The theological meaning is 'the taking away of sin or the complete satisfaction for our sin.' Only the Lord Jesus Christ could make full satisfaction for our sin."*[9]

Sacrifices Simply Pointed To, But Did Not Fulfill
It seems pretty clear to me that the teaching is *not* about the Old Testament sacrifices *removing* anything. It is about them *pointing* to their actual fulfillment in Jesus Christ. The OT sacrificial system did *not* provide salvation. It was a *precursor* to it, merely pointing to the One who came to be the ultimate, final, and once-for-all sacrifice.

I hope that the reader agrees that nothing written so far is teaching that there is another salvation *apart* from Jesus Christ, or that at one point salvation was by grace *and* works, later to be changed to grace *alone*. Salvation was *never* by grace and works. It was *always* (and remains) based on faith. This is the difficulty with Covenant Theology, because many within this system firmly believe that for Adam and Eve, this alleged Covenant of Works was one that required them to *do* something in order to obtain salvation. Tragically, this detracts from God's solution, in which He and He alone did what He required in order that salvation could be extended. There is nothing that man does in order to work for, or in any way earn, salvation (cf. Ephesians 2:8-10). Salvation is an absolute gift, with no strings attached. Had Adam and Eve continued to believe God's veracity, there would have been no failure to obey and no resultant fallen nature.

Human Government
The Dispensation of Conscience continued for a while and in fact, it

---
[9] Ibid, 1

should be noted that it continues to this day! The new information or responsibilities of one particular dispensation do not necessarily swallow up, replace, or delete the ones, which come after it.

Beginning with Genesis 8:20, we see that God is most definitely instituting something new: the *death penalty*. While it could be argued that God instituted the death penalty when He killed some animals to cover Adam's and Eve's sin, the death penalty we are referring to here is the one which God directed toward man, when one person attacks another with the intent to take the other's life.

During this dispensation, the Holy Spirit continued to use man's conscience to instruct man and attempt to keep him obedient, but now something greater was needed, due to what can only be described as the absolute corruption of humanity. God needed to induce *fear* as a reason *not* do something. Capital punishment was instituted by God for a few reasons, both of which are delineated in Genesis 8. God wanted people to think twice and even three times or more before they took another's life in malice or anger. Self-defense is one thing, but God is not speaking to Noah about self-defense here. He is speaking of the deliberate taking of another person's life out of hate, convenience, malice, or pre-planning.

Ultimately, to kill another individual is to literally strike out at God, because man was *made* in God's image. I find it fascinating that evolution, by its very nature, teaches through implication that man is valueless. We evolved from some bacteria, proteins and other things and here we are today. God says the exact opposite. We are supremely valuable because we were made in God's image. Christ's voluntary life, death, and resurrection are proof enough of this. If man had no value, would God be willing to go through all He went through as God the Son, dying a brutally horrific death, shedding His blood in order that sin – your sin and mine – would once and for all be cancelled?

We learned from the Creation account that man was made in God's image. That part is not new. What *is* new is that man is now given the responsibility of using capital punishment to execute those who strike out at God by killing another person. This is the new information, *progressively* revealed by God during this age, which was not given before. Prior to this, man was not commanded to use the death penalty. This is newly revealed information, but again has nothing to do with salvation and everything to do with God's progressively revealed plans and purposes.

Cain
We are all aware that Cain was the first human being to take another human being's life. However, there was no law prohibiting it. Certainly, Cain's conscience (if it still worked) would have attempted to dissuade him from doing harm to his brother Abel, but it was overruled by his jealousy, which gave birth to rage. That rage, just as James says in the New Testament, went unchecked and brought about death: the death of Abel. We read about these two brothers and Abel's murder in Genesis 4.

In full-blown, uncontrolled fury, Cain attacks and kills his own brother. Why? In chapter four of Genesis, we learn that Cain brought the fruit of the field as a sacrifice to God, while his brother Abel brought meat from his herd as an offering. I am going to ask that the reader to please pay very close attention to what is coming next.

As noted, it is important to note that the sacrificial system was obviously a normal part of life at this point. God had instructed our first parents, and they in turn had obviously instructed *their* children. Both Cain and Abel knew of this sacrificial system and its necessity by virtue of the fact that they were using it. They did not create it out of some superstitious system of belief. They were directly *taught* to use it by their parents and were undoubtedly given instruction as to *why* its use was necessary.

Believing Equals Salvation

Why was Cain's offering refused, while Abel's was not? If we are not careful, we can make the mistake of focusing on the *type* of sacrifice, or the action (or *work* itself) of each brother. Put another way, we can focus on the *work*, or *effort*, of Cain and Abel, while losing sight of the *meaning* behind it. It is clear from the text in Genesis 4 that Abel observably brought the correct offering. Cain did not. End of story, right? Wrong. There is something far deeper here.

Cain brought the wrong offering and this was *solely* because he really did not care if he pleased God at all. He did not *believe* he needed to do so. This complete lack of *believing* on Cain's part, related to God's instructions about sacrifices. In essence, he did *not* believe his parents when they told him about God and what God required. Cain did not have the necessary *faith* in God to begin with, and *this* is why he brought the wrong offering. He simply did not care enough to believe God in the first place. He figured, "*All I have are fruits and vegetables. Oh well. Whatever. Just want to get this done! Why we have to do this is beyond me anyway. Ridiculous!*"

Instead of going to Abel and purchasing (or trading for) animals to have the proper offering, Cain said "*Forget it, I'm not going to go to that trouble. Abel thinks he's so great anyway, I'm not going to give him any more reason to believe it! God gets what I have and if that does not make Him happy, that's life, if God exists at all!*"

I'm sure you see what is going on here. It was not so much that Cain's *offering* was rejected by God. It was Cain *himself* and his *attitude*, which God rejected out of hand. The act of bringing the wrong offering to sacrifice is no different from Adam and Eve "bringing" the wrong attitude when it came time to deal with the forbidden fruit they were to ignore. All three: Adam, Eve, and Cain *failed* in their attitudes.

Cain did not *believe* God when he was told that the offerings should be specific, and it showed in his *actions*. On the other hand, Abel *believed* God and it showed in *his* actions. The difference is stark and the type of offering that each brought is simply symptomatic of what they *believed* about God to begin with, and whether or not they believed God at all. Their believing is what allowed God to count them righteous, by His *grace*, looking ahead to the cross.

It Begins and Ends with Faith
Salvation for Cain and Abel was *not* found in the type of offering they presented to God. Salvation either came or did not come before that offering was presented. Salvation was found in whether or not they *believed* God's initial Word to Adam and Eve. *That* is what provided their salvation.

It should be getting easier to see that starting with Adam and Eve and continuing from there, it is *faith, faith, FAITH* in God's *Word* that brings salvation from God to the individual. Without faith, there is no pleasing God at all (Hebrews 11:6). *With* faith, God is well pleased. With faith, the individual *does* what is *right* in God's sight. Cain did not do what was right in God's sight because he did not *believe* God's Word (regarding the correct sacrifices to bring). Cain was devoid of faith where God was concerned. He did not have God's salvation at all (cf. Mark 11:22; Romans 1:17, 4:20, 5:2; Galatians 3:11, 3:26; Ephesians 6:23; I Peter 1:21).

Just as Adam and Eve chose to believe the Tempter and reject God as Truth, Cain follows their example of unbelief. His actions followed his unbelief, as Adam's and Eve's actions followed *their* unbelief. The difference of course, is that it is very likely that Adam and Eve *did become* saved, because they took seriously the institution of the sacrificial system (later refined under Moses, and perfected and fulfilled through Christ). We know this because of how they instructed their sons, Cain and Abel. We know that at least Abel "got it," and understood that the right offering stemmed from the right attitude.

By the time we get to Noah, the sacrificial system had been well established and in use for some time. It should be clear that even though the Dispensationalist calls the era after the Flood the age of Human Government; this simply defines the *specific additional responsibilities* of that particular dispensation.

After the Flood, God told Noah that whoever kills another, God would "require [the murderer's] lifeblood" (Genesis 9:5). This is the new addition for this particular age of Human Government. From that time on, murderers were supposed to be put to death. God has never rescinded that rule, either.

However, what about salvation here? Is it different? Has anything with respect to salvation *changed*? No. Salvation came by faith for Adam and Eve. It came by faith during Noah's day as well.

Notice in Genesis chapter eight that the ark with Noah and his family came to rest on one of the mountains of Ararat. When the waters had receded far enough, the people and animals exited the ark. God then repeated what He had told Adam and Eve centuries before about being fruitful and multiplying, and filling the earth (cf. Genesis 8:17). Life was then to begin again. Noah and his children were to replenish the earth with people. Certainly, the animals would do that and would find their place in various parts of the world.

Noah Worships God
One of the first things Noah did after exiting the ark was to build an altar upon which he offered clean animals as a sacrifice to God. Did Noah have to do this in order to receive salvation? No. He did it for the sole purpose of *worshiping* God. This was an act of worship and adoration for God's providential care for Noah and his family, and all the animals. This had *nothing* to do with obtaining salvation; nothing at all. Noah had already been *declared* righteous by God before the Flood, which was why God was able to save him and his family at all (cf. Genesis 6).

Noah was declared righteous by God because he *believed* God. When God told Noah that He was going to destroy the earth and that he should begin building an ark, Noah did exactly that! He *did* it because he *believed* God, taking Him at His Word. There seemed to be no hesitation on Noah's part where God was concerned.

Noah had obviously believed God prior to this as well, because the text essentially tells us that besides Noah, there was not one other righteous person on the face of the earth. Noah (and his family) was spared because of this righteousness. Please understand that this righteousness was *imputed* (credited to a person's account) by God. That was done because of Noah's *belief*. It is also noteworthy to point out that this believing in God had created a pattern of living that pleased God. However, note that Noah's pattern of living *began* because of what he *believed* about God, long before the Flood. The believing came *first*. It was routinely followed by the correct *action*.

When Noah worshipped through those offerings after exiting the Ark, God received Noah's worship and promised him that He would never destroy the earth again with a flood. He placed the rainbow in the sky as a reminder of that covenant. Certainly, this can be called a covenant from God, and it was *unconditional* in nature, by the way. Man had to do nothing. God did it all and we still continue to see the rainbow in the sky after it rains, in spite of the fact that man continues to blaspheme God on a daily basis (even going so far as to take the rainbow and using it to represent a lifestyle that is diametrically opposed to God and the way He has set up humanity to live). Nevertheless, God chose back during Noah's time never again to destroy the earth with a global flood, and He has kept, and will continue to keep that promise because we have seen that God cannot lie.

That Sounds Promising
Beginning in chapter twelve of Genesis, another age begins. This age has as its central figure a man named Abraham (originally Abram). It

was during this period that God made certain specific promises to Abraham, which we will spend a bit of time considering.

Before we do though, we need to note that God had not *negated* anything He had previously placed into effect before Abraham. The Holy Spirit continued to use man's conscience to convict. The death penalty was still in full force. The rainbow would still be seen in the sky after it rained. The *addition* to this particular age is found in the set of *promises* that God made to Abraham. It is here that we begin to see more concrete signs of the actual salvific plan that would be made available to humanity through the sacrificial death and resurrection of Jesus Christ.

What God revealed to Abraham then was by way of *progressively revealing* more information to him about the coming Messiah who would in turn become the Lamb slain for the forgiveness of sins. Has the plan of salvation always been the same? Of course. God merely chose to *reveal* it in steps over time, but the major component was always in place: *faith in God's Word.* The plan never, *ever* changed. It was decided in eternity past, in the council of the Godhead, but the *knowledge of it* was revealed little by little *to* man. Please remember that salvation has always been by faith in God.

In Genesis 12:1-3, we read *"Now the Lord said to Abram, 'Go forth from your country, and from your father's relatives and from your father's house, to the land which I will show you; and I will make you a great nation, and I will bless you, and make your name great; and so you shall be a blessing; and I will bless those who bless you, and the one who curses you I will curse. And in you all the families of the earth shall be blessed."*

Notice that God promised Abram that He would:

1. Make Abraham into a great nation
2. Make Abraham's name great

3. Bless all the families of the earth through Abraham

This is the new addition to this new dispensation. Regardless of what some would like to insist, God had never mentioned any of this before in any portion of Scripture prior to Genesis 12. He alluded to the larger picture of salvation that would come through the woman's Seed and Satan's seed (in Genesis 3), but there were very few details at all associated with God's first announcement. God took His own, deliberate time to reveal the specifics of that plan. What man knew was that faith was needed. That had been settled once for all. From there, God gave a little information here, a bit more there, still more there, until we get to Jesus and His death and resurrection thousands of years later.

Take a moment and try to imagine how Satan would have prepared for Christ's First Coming, His entire life, His death, and His resurrection had he known all the details thousands of years before it happened! God never let that happen since He provided information on a *need to know* basis. Satan simply did not need to know and neither did man. What man needed to do was trust God and in due time, things would come into focus. Satan was just as stymied, but he had no way to please the Lord as man did, by evidencing faith in Him. Amen, Lord!

How anyone can read the Bible and *not* see a progressive revelation of God's will at work is remarkable. At the same time, how tragic that the folks who are unable to see that progression condemn as heretical those *do* see it. It appears that the problem may well have to do with the fact that they see the full spectrum of God's will *only* in terms of salvation.

We have seen that the major element of salvation was already in place from the very beginning: *faith*. The sacrificial system, which came afterwards, did not provide salvation. It merely pointed to that one, perfect sacrifice in Jesus Christ. These sacrifices by Adam and

Eve, Abel, Noah, and the rest were to *teach* them of the coming absolute sacrifice. It was almost as if the sacrifices in the OT were done as a memorial of what *would be*, much as we take part of the Lord's Supper today as a memorial of what Christ *accomplished*. Certainly, the Old Testament sacrificial system was a precursor to that perfect sacrifice of Jesus Christ.

These promises God made to Abraham are *unconditional* in nature and this is the first time God reveals this part of His overall plan to anyone at all. Some argue that these promises *to*, or covenants *with*, Abraham were *conditional* in nature. However, this is untrue. There is nothing in the text where God says anything like *"Abraham, here is what I am going to do for you. Here is what you will need to do for me in order to keep this covenant in place."* Nothing exists within the text, which would indicate that God's promises to Abraham were based on something Abraham would do.

In fact, it appears to be an open and shut case in Hebrews 11, which states *"By faith Abraham, when he was tested, offered up Isaac, and he who had received the promises was in the act of offering up his only son"* (Hebrews 11:17; cf. Hebrews 7:6). The text states that Abraham received the promises, and please note that this is *past* tense. Abraham had already received the promises, and they were not based on Abraham giving up his only son here. In fact, we are told in Hebrews 6:15 that all Abraham had to do was wait patiently. In this same chapter, beginning with verse 13 to 14, we read *"For when God made a promise to Abraham, since he had no one greater by whom to swear, he swore by himself, saying, 'Surely I will bless you and multiply you'."*

Note that God was making a promise to Abraham, and chapter six of Hebrews goes onto explain that when people make a promise to another person they will usually "swear" by something greater than themselves. However, God had no one He could look to who was greater, so He swore by Himself to Abraham that what He was promising, He would fulfill.

The writer of Hebrews finishes these thoughts by adding, "*So when God desired to show more convincingly to the heirs of the promise the unchangeable character of his purpose, he guaranteed it with an oath, so that by two unchangeable things, in which it is impossible for God to lie, we who have fled for refuge might have strong encouragement to hold fast to the hope set before us*" (Hebrews 6:17-18).

What this is clearly stating is that:

- *God made the promises originally to Abraham*
- *God swore by Himself that He would keep His promises*
- *God convinced Abraham's heirs of the same promise with an oath, guaranteeing that what He promised would occur*
- *God does not change*
- *God cannot lie*

In God's threefold promise to Abraham, we see His intentions to make Abraham a great nation, to make his name great, and to bless all the families of the earth *through* Abraham. We see throughout God's dealings with Abraham and his heirs that God continued to remind them of His *original* promises to Abraham. God does not change. He does not lie. He brings about what He promises.

Looking at the world today, we see that what God promised Israel has *not* come about in its entirety. Has God changed His mind? No, because He says He cannot do that. Did He lie? No, He cannot lie because that is against His nature. Was God not able to see when He first called Abraham and promised to him the things that He would do, that Israel would eventually *reject* the Messiah? Of course, He saw that, from eternity past. If He saw that even then, yet made the unalterable promises *to* Abraham and to his descendents, how is it possible that Israel exists as it does today, with yet unfulfilled promises?

There are only two possible conclusions. Either:

1. *God still has unfinished work with Israel, because of Abraham, or*
2. *Israel has been replaced by the Church.*

However, if God's promises to Abraham were *unconditional* in nature, God has absolutely no wiggle room to take Israel out of the picture and transfer anything to the Church. To do so would require God to break His promises and we have already learned that He is unable to lie.

If, on the other hand, His promises *could* be broken by Abraham or any of his descendents, then it would be possible for God to remove Israel permanently out of the picture, replacing her with the Church. Determining which scenario is accurate is obviously extremely important. This cannot be left up to guesswork or chance. Either God has provided His plan with clarity or He has not. It is up to us to seek the truth that He has provided in His Word.

How can we determine the nature of God's promises to Abraham and his heirs? If God's promises were *conditional*, something would have been required of Abraham. If they were *unconditional*, nothing would have been required of Abraham. It is as simple as that. One need only determine if God's promises to Abraham were of a condition or unconditional nature, and then the answer pertaining to whether Israel has any future with God becomes apparent. An in order to resolve this, we need look no further than the text.

The only thing required of Abraham was to "go." He was to leave his family and go to the land that God would show him. That was it. End of story. However, even if we agree that this covenant *was* conditional (which we do not), it is clear from the text that Abraham obeyed God by "going forth from [his] country." God said "Go" and Abraham "went." If that is a *condition*, then Abraham fulfilled it (cf. Genesis 12:1-3).

Genesis 12:4 states quite clearly, *"So Abram went, as the LORD had told him, and Lot went with him. Abram was seventy-five years old when he departed from Haran."* There can be no doubt then that what Abraham was required to do was done. God said "go" and Abraham "went."

Someone might argue that Abraham did not really obey God to the letter. God had specifically stated *"Go from your country and your kindred and your father's house to the land that I will show you"* (Genesis 12:1). Did Abraham actually leave his kindred and his father's house? Abraham took Lot (his nephew; cf. Genesis 12:5). He also took his own wife, Sarah. Beyond that, he took all of his possessions, *"and the people that they had acquired in Haran"* (Genesis 12:5). If someone wants to be a legalist, then it may be that Abraham did not follow God to the letter. However, God's instructions were to "go from your kindred and your father's house..." Do we actually know how specific that was for Abraham? Surely, God did not expect Abraham to leave his wife, or their possessions behind. Similarly, taking Lot seemed permissible as did taking all the other people who were part of Abraham's household. While Lot caused a bit of a problem for Abraham later on, there seems to be nothing in the text that would indicate God's displeasure.

In fact, once Abraham and his household crossed into Canaan and through to Shechem, we read, *"To your offspring I will give this land"* (Genesis 12:7). We do not read anything that even remotely appears to be remonstration from the Lord, which we might expect had Abraham not followed the Lord's directive by taking Lot.

In fact, it seems clear from the text that when God approached Abraham initially, He gave him a *directive*. He did NOT say "Abraham, IF you go, I will do such and such..." He said, "Abraham, GO!" Abraham went. So even if it can be argued that this was a conditional covenant, given to Abraham by God, it is clear from the text that Abraham obeyed God, thereby fulfilling his end of the covenant. Since Abraham actually left his land to go to the land that God would give his descendents, then it is very safe to say that anything conditioned upon Abraham's obedience was fully met.

It was this act of obedience, which stemmed from the fact that Abraham *believed* God when God revealed part of His plan for Abraham. God said it and Abraham believed it. This is where righteousness begins: in the will of each individual. Abraham did what he was told because he had absolutely no reason to doubt God's Word. It was his belief in God that allowed righteousness to be *credited to him*.. His obedience, which *followed*, was the *result* of his believing God.

Kids Today...

This is no different from when God laid down the law with Adam and Eve. He gave them one *rule* and expected it to be followed. He of course knew that it would *not* be followed. Nonetheless, he gave them the rule that was to be the guideline for their behavior in the Garden of Eden. They were to believe God in everything He stated to them.

Parents give their kids rules all the time. *"Jimmy, I want that grass mowed by the time I get home, all right? And do not use the gas in the can marked "Edger" because that gas has oil mixed with it. It will ruin the mower if you use that gas."*

So the dad provided Jimmy with all the information he needs:

- Mow the grass by the time he arrives home
- Do not use the wrong gas can

No one would say that Dad entered into a covenant Jimmy! That would be absurd. When parents lay down the law with their children, it is generally *not* known as a covenant! It is known as *the law*. Yes, there are negative consequences of not following the law as laid down by the parent. Any positive consequences are merely implied. However, because Jimmy really has no alternative but to obey, it is not considered a covenant. Sure, Jimmy can decide *not* to obey, and the consequences of that would vary from household to household. However, the point is that by simply obeying his father, Jimmy's relationship with Dad will remain the same. Jimmy really has no option to disagree. Dad has removed that decision from him.

If Jimmy does everything his dad said, everything would be fine. No worries. Dad might come home and say *"Great job on the lawn, Jimmy! Thank you for doing what I asked."* Dad might come home and say nothing at all, but merely continue to love his son, spending time with him after dinner, helping him with his homework, or something else.

If Jimmy either did not mow the lawn, or used the wrong gas and ruined the lawn mower, there would be problems. However, it is seriously doubtful that Jimmy would be *disowned* because of it. He might be grounded, or his gaming systems might be taken away, or both. He also might be expected to pay for the repairs to the mower. Any number of things could take place. His obedience (or not) would depend upon his attitude towards his father.

We see this perfectly played out in the parable of the Prodigal Son, recorded for us in Luke 15:11-32. In this story, we read of a father who loved both of his sons. They both did the work they were required to do by their father; however, the younger had grown extremely tired and frustrated with all the work that his father made him do. He wanted out.

Scripture tells us that he went to his father and said, *"Father, give me the share of property that is coming to me"* (Luke 15:12). The first thing that is interesting here is that the younger son was essentially asking for his inheritance while his father was still alive. Normally, people do not inherit anything until the person who is leaving that inheritance has died. The son did not feel like waiting, so he had the gall to ask his father for his inheritance right then.

Without an argument, the father gave the younger son what he requested and without so much as a "thanks Dad!", the son was off to start a new life. I like the way John MacArthur describes this situation: *"[The younger son] wanted whatever he could get* now, *chiefly because he needed it to finance his rebellion. He didn't want any responsibility that came with the inheritance. He wanted no part in the ongoing management of the estate. In fact, what he seems to have wanted most of all was to get rid of the duties, the expectations, and the stewardship that came with being the son of such a successful man."*[10]

That is it exactly. The younger son was like many of us: we want someone to finance our rebellion! We want the cash, with no responsibilities attached to it. This son took what he did not want to wait for (and the father did *not* have to give), and left home in search of places and ways to sow his wild oats. He soon found plenty of opportunities to do so.

Eventually though, this younger son came up against the same brick wall that all people in that situation come against: *cash flow*. Things certainly started out fine enough. He had money and quite a bit of it and people noticed. They began to hang around him because he was their "sugar daddy," allowing them to participate in his exploits without their having to open up their own wallets. Unfortunately, for the younger son, he did not realize *why* they liked him until after all of his money was gone. His reckless living days were over. The Scripture says, *"when he had spent everything, a severe famine arose in that country, and he began to be in need"* (Luke 15:14). Since he was not taking in or earning any money (because he was not working, but simply playing), it was inevitable that his money would run out eventually.

---

[10] John MacArthur *A Tale of Two Sons* (Nashville: Thomas Nelson 2008), 49

Because of a severe famine that hit the land, he did the only thing he thought he could do and *"he went and hired himself out to one of the citizens of that country, who sent him into his fields to feed pigs. And he was longing to be fed with the pods that the pigs ate, and no one gave him anything"* (Luke 15:15-16). Here he was so hungry that he was willing to eat what he was feeding the pigs. If you couple this with the fact that this young man was Jewish, and went to "a far country" which was in all likelihood Gentile, his job of feeding pigs becomes even more intolerable. Here he was, the younger son of a successful Jewish businessman, who wanted nothing more than to "get his share'" and take off at a run to a new life.

The situation caught up with him though, when he ran out of money and wound up working in a situation that was considered unclean by Jewish standards: working with pigs. He did this for a while, until he finally came to his senses. It was almost as if the light came on above his head. He realized that if he was working, he might as well be working at home, on his father's estate. He knew that, at the very least, those who worked for his father *"have more than enough bread, but I perish here with hunger! I will arise and go to my father, and I will say to him, 'Father, I have sinned against heaven and before you"* (Luke 15:17-18). In fact, he felt bad enough to realize that because of his reprehensible behavior, his father had every right to disassociate himself with him.

He decided to go back to his father, confess his sin, and then beg his father to allow him to come back as a hired servant, to be treated no better than any of them. His father though, had other plans.

It is interesting that the biblical text states *"But while he was still a long way off, his father saw him and felt compassion, and ran and embraced him and kissed him"* (Luke 15:20). Such love that the father had for his son; not unlike our heavenly Father who has infinitely more love for His children.

While the son was willing to return only as a paid servant, his father would have none of it. He ordered the robe and ring to be brought and the fattened calf slaughtered because this was a very special occasion: *"For this my son was dead, and is alive again; he was lost, and is found"* (Luke 15:24).

We see that this father's love was such that even the disobedience and rebellion of his youngest could not squelch that love. His love for his children was stalwart, steady, and eternal. This father is a picture of God and the way He views us, His children. This fact makes it that much more difficult to comprehend some who espouse that God has forever written off Israel because of their rejection of the Messiah.

However, notice though, that in this story the father went beyond the call of duty. He did not have to give his son anything at all, even *after* he had died, but he did. To make matters worse, the son took the money and ran, leaving his father to explain to everyone where his son went and why. He would also likely have had to face questions as to why he had not publicly disowned his son because of his actions. The father's love was such that he did not disown him, and it appears from the narrative that he may have looked to the horizon on a daily basis to see if his son was returning. The only covenant that existed between the father and son was a covenant of love. While the father would not stop his son from making decisions that might end badly, he would not stop loving him either. As difficult as it was for him to watch and bear, the father knew that life's best examples were often learned the hard way.

There was no guarantee to the son that his unwise decision would not cost him dearly, but the father – because of his love – allowed him to make his own choice and trusted that he would return one day, an older, wiser man. This man would understand with what love the father loved him.

So it was with Adam and Eve, that there was no spoken guarantee to them that good things would happen if they continued to ignore the forbidden tree. However, the implication or assumption was that to ignore the fruit would mean that life would continue as it had. They probably could not have imagined anything better than the situation they found themselves already living in anyway.

What would God say to them? *"If you ignore the tree for x-amount of days, I will give you something you will really like! I will make the trees larger and the fruit sweeter!"* I cannot imagine God saying anything that would present a better picture of life for them. They were simply required to obey God. That obedience would allow life to continue as it had. That obedience would result in a continued belief that God had told them the truth.

As far as they knew, they were already going to live forever. They enjoyed perfect health. They were not afraid of any creature and there was no creature that was afraid of them. Every creature – man and animal – was vegetarian at that point, requiring nothing to be slaughtered for food. What could God possibly tell them that would benefit them more?

God merely told them that they had to keep *one* law. To keep it would mean (to them) continuing as they already existed. To ignore it meant *death*. This is what they had been told and it was up to them to believe it or not.

When the enemy came to them in the cool of the garden, he prompted them to question God's truthfulness. When God gave them the command not to eat of the fruit that grew on that particular tree, there is nothing in the text indicating *why* God created that tree, placed it in the garden, and then required them to avoid it. All God had said was, *"You may surely eat of every tree of the garden, but of the tree of the knowledge of good and evil you shall not eat, for in the day that you eat of it you shall surely die"* (Genesis 2:16-17).

There is nothing in there that unveils God's reason for making the fruit of that tree off limits. They chose not to question Him either. It was a rule they were to simply obey. They did, for a while at least.

When the Tempter, in the form of the serpent, came to them, he pointedly called God a lair and then provided a *reason* why God had given them that rule in the first place. It amounted to God being a jealous God, not wanting to share certain insights and knowledge with His creation. The Tempter stated, "*You will not surely die. For God knows that when you eat of it your eyes will be opened, and you will be like God, knowing good and evil*" (Genesis 3:4b-5).

How do you like that? Satan came along, told them directly that they would *not* die, and then stated that their eyes would be opened to the knowledge of good and evil. He was half-right. They *did* die spiritually, and they *began* to die physically. They also now knew experientially the difference between good and evil, something God would likely have given them knowledge of *without* having had to actually sin, had they not heeded the voice of the Tempter.

Again, any covenant with Adam and Eve is lacking here. God gave them a directive and He expected it to be obeyed. They obeyed for a time, then gave in to the snare of the Tempter and wound up disobeying.

A father tells his children not to climb up the tree next to the house because it is old and rotting and needs to be taken down. For a time, the children obey, dutifully avoiding said tree. It is still in their backyard, but they move around it as if it is not there.

However, one day, a friend comes over and they are now all playing in the backyard. The friend is used to climbing up that tree with the children because they had done it so many times before. Now though, the children warn him that their father has said they must avoid the tree because it is old and filled with rot and soon to be cut down.

The boy, hanging from the lower limb, looks up into the tree. To him, it is nothing but a wooden jungle gym that he has climbed on many times before. He says as much to the children, chiding them for being afraid to climb the tree. He cajoles and insists that they follow him up to the top. The children, bewildered, look at one another, then slowly move toward the tree, as they watch their friend continue to climb to the top.

As the children reach the bottom branches, they hear a loud 'crack' from above them. They look up to see their friend hurtling to the ground, holding part of a branch that broke off from the tree. Their friend lands with a sickening "thud." No one moves and time seems to stand still.

The children look at the boy who is not moving, but still breathing. Together, they both run into the house yelling for their mother, who comes running out of the house to see the fallen boy. Emergency services are called; they arrive and take the boy to the hospital. He will live, but has some nasty bruises, a few cracked ribs and a broken arm for his trouble; all because he did not think it was important enough to listen to the children.

When the father told his children to avoid the tree, did he make a covenant with them? Of course not. He gave them a directive - an order - a rule to live by until that tree was removed from their property. To obey the father meant they would not get hurt. To ignore the father and continue to play on the tree meant the real possibility of being hurt or killed.

Moses: Another Example
The life of Moses also provides many examples for us regarding God's promises, directives, and covenants. One in particular is found in Ex-

odus 4. Here, God spoke to Moses and He essentially told Moses to *"Go and tell Pharaoh to release the children of Israel."* This was *in no way* a covenant. It was a *directive* and Moses did his level best to squeak out from underneath it, using every excuse he could find. At each turn, God said, *"Sorry, Moses. I've chosen you."* Finally, after the last excuse Moses provided, God said, *"Okay, I've had it. Take your brother Aaron with you then. He will be your spokesman, but YOU are going!"* Moses went.

This was not a covenant God had entered into with Moses. God gave Moses an order - a directive - something to be obeyed. In this case, God was not taking "no" for an answer.

Remember, nowhere has God changed His salvation for humanity. He has simply chosen to reveal aspects of it *progressively*. Did Moses know nothing about God's intentions to create the nation of Israel? Was he aware that a Messiah would come from that nation? Was Moses aware that many of the things he did were *types* for Christ? He probably did quite a few things out of simple obedience without fully knowing what they may have stood for at the time. Many aspects of God's plans and purposes are revealed only in their proper time.

Mosaic Law

In Exodus 19, we read the narrative of God presenting Moses with the Ten Commandments. Since this is the first time that the Ten Commandments had been given (along with the other Jewish laws), it also clearly ushers in a new dispensation. Normally, the name associated with this particular age is the Mosaic Law, or the Law. God's salvation had not changed. Faith was still required in order to be found favorable in His sight. However, responsibilities that are more specific were given to His nation of Israel, by which they might become familiar with the sacrificial system and the ceremonial and dietary laws that would keep them healthy.

God, through the Holy Spirit, was still using man's conscience here to restrain and indict him. Human government was still in place. It was still a crime punishable by death when someone maliciously killed another. In fact, God elaborates on this and other laws. We continue to see the presence of the Abrahamic Covenant in the creation of the nation of Israel under Moses. In fact, there is nothing that would indicate that God had rescinded any portion of the promises He had originally made to Abraham.

Now though, God adds *another* form of responsibility, further revealing another portion of His plan: Ten Commandments and the other laws. This particular area of responsibility was given *only* to the nation of Israel. No other civilization or culture that existed at that time was partnered with Israel here.

Alva McClain states this about the Ten Commandments, "*the blessings of the law were conditional, dependent upon Israel's obedience.*"[11] Notice that it is the *blessings,* which were conditional, *not* salvation. As long as they kept God's commands, life would be well with them. When they sinned through any form of rebellion, the blessings would be removed from Israel. We see this repeatedly throughout the Old Testament. Israel sinned by rebelling, and God sent judgment, usually in the form of an invasion by a neighboring empire. The cities of Israel were pillaged and plundered and the people were either killed, taken as slaves, or both. This was God's way of getting Israel's attention so that they could clearly see that the blessings were gone because they had turned away from God.

Is it any different for the Christian? Some of us are very wayward people, but thankfully God will "never leave or forsake" us (cf. John 6:37; John 10:28; Hebrews 13:5). This promise by God in Christ is for our comfort, because it gives us hope that when we *do* temporarily fall away through sin God is still there waiting for us when we get

---

[11] Alva J. McClain *Law and Grace* (Winona Lake: BMH Books 2008), 32

back up. This is no different from the prodigal's father, who waited anxiously to see his son on the distant horizon daily.

However, some may say that Dispensationalism teaches that this applies to Christians only because Dispensationalism teaches that Christians are under the age of Grace. This is in fact, *not* what Dispensationalism teaches. In fact, Dispensationalism understands quite clearly that *everything* God did, and in *every* way in which He dealt with humanity, *grace* was the overriding factor. It was all grace, and it was all based on His promises to us.

Nevertheless, the Old Testament provides a picture of God's faithfulness, which is also solely based on His grace. I Samuel 12:22 states, *"For the LORD will not forsake his people, for his great name's sake, because it has pleased the LORD to make you a people for himself."* Here, the reference is to Israel, the Jewish people, whom God referred to as the apple of His eye. Zechariah states, *"For thus said the LORD of hosts, after his glory sent me to the nations who plundered you, for he who touches you touches the apple of his eye"* (Zechariah 2:8).

Regarding this Mosaic Law age, has salvation changed with this new dispensation? No, and we can clearly see that the sacrificial system was still present, though God had refined and elaborated on it. This sacrificial system, as stated previously, did *not* obtain salvation for the one offering the sacrifice. It *identified* the person sacrificing the animal(s) with the person's sin. It continued to point to the all-sufficiency of Jesus Christ's one-time, final offering of Himself on Calvary's cross.

Once again, it is by faith that an individual's offering is accepted or not; not the correctness of the offering itself. He receives those who approach God in faith. The faith that they exhibit, which results in right actions, is the sole evidence of their believing God. This He then counts as righteousness, by "crediting" the individual with the righteousness that would come from the cross, even though yet future. God was able to count their faith as righteousness because of the fact that the cross of Jesus Christ *would* occur. Since God is outside the dimension of time, the cross is always before Him.

Grace: *Always* Present

Following the age (or dispensation) of the Mosaic Law, we move into the area of Grace, which takes the stage in the New Testament. This is also where many people get the impression that the Dispensationalist does *not* believe that grace was present during these other dispensations. Since he does not believe that grace was apparent or operative during the previous dispensations, then salvation must have come by works. This is simply untrue, and it is hoped that everything shown thus far has served to eradicate this error.

Let us be clear here: Grace was *always* an important and prevalent aspect of anything God did with humanity. Without it, He would have destroyed *all* men, saving no one. We would not be here today, reading this book, or studying His Word. Had grace not been an absolute part of all of God's dealings with humanity, God could not have worked with us at all. Works simply would not have cut it, since our works amount to nothing.

There was one other important benefit during this period of Mosaic Law. This actually and officially began with Christ's atonement on Calvary's cross and His eventual ascension, and that is the *indwelling* presence of the Holy Spirit. This is something that the saints of the Old Testament did not have on a regular or permanent basis. The Holy Spirit might come upon someone and could just as easily leave him or her. This needs to be explained before we move on.

The Holy Spirit had a number of ministries to Old Testament saints: 1) regeneration, 2) selective indwelling, 3) restraining sin, and 4) enabling for service.

The regeneration aspect of the Holy Spirit's work related to an individual's salvation. According to Enns, *"In Ezekiel 18:31 the people were commanded to 'make yourselves a new heart and a new spirit.' The two phrases parallel those of Ezekiel 36:25-27 as well as John 3:5 and suggest the Old Testament believer was regenerated by the Holy Spirit (cf. also Ps. 51:10)."*[12] Regeneration has to do with salvation and it cannot happen without the Holy Spirit's involvement.

The *mode* of saving the Old Testament saint was the same then as it is now: *faith*. It was their faith in God that allowed them to receive salvation. Their belief in God allowed Him to identify them as righteous based on their faith, just as today Christians are declared righteous based on their faith in God. There is absolutely no difference in the way people were saved during the Old Testament times, the New Testament times, and today.

The other services performed by the Holy Spirit in and through the Old Testament saint were not necessarily permanent. This is understood from passages such as John 14:16-17, when Jesus spoke of Pentecost and the results of it. This permanent indwelling of the Holy Spirit was for service, and growth toward maturity in Christ for the New Testament saint. The Old Testament saints, while regenerated as the same Holy Spirit regenerates us, were often endowed with specific gifts by the Holy Spirit for specific tasks. Once the task was completed, that particular gift might be withdrawn (cf. Judges 3:10; 6:34; 11:29; 14:6; Numbers 24:2; I Samuel 10:10; 16:14, etc.).

Millennium
The last age or dispensation normally taught within the Dispensational model is called the Dispensation of the Millennium simply because it reflects that particular period the period in which Jesus reigns physically and literally on the earth for a time of 1,000 years

---

[12] Paul Enns *Moody Handbook of Theology* (Chicago: Moody Press 1989), 260

from Jerusalem. This particular dispensation is referenced in Revelation 20:1-15.

Ryrie indicates that the responsibilities of man during this time are to *"believe and obey Christ and His government."*[13]

It is not the intention of this book to deal with prophecy, though we will touch on certain aspects of it. I mention it here simply because it is part of the landscape of Dispensationalism.

We have seen the various ages or dispensations espoused by Dispensationalism. The names of each age may vary, but in general, the truth or content within each age has been explained here. The most important thing to understand is that though the dispensations differ from one another regarding the responsibilities of man, salvation does *not*. This author believes that Ryrie and others have successfully countered the charges put forth by detractors of Dispensationalism. Unfortunately, the charges persist, likely due to either an unwillingness or inability to hear and digest the counter-arguments espoused by Ryrie, et al.

Commenting on this situation, Ryrie states, *"The charge that dispensationalism teaches multiple ways of salvation is repeated with the regularity of a dripping faucet. John Wick Bowman declared in 1965, 'If any man is saved in any dispensation other than those of Promise and Grace, he is saved by* works *and not faith! [The dispensationalist] is clearly left with two methods of salvation on his hands – works for the majority of dispensations, faith for the rest – and we have to deal with a fickle God who deals with man in various ways at various times'."*[14]

Of course, this is nothing less than unfortunate because it is obvious that Bowman is confusing God's progressively revealed plans and

---

[13] Charles C. Ryrie *Dispensationalism Revised & Expanded* (Chicago: Moody 2007), 62
[14] Charles C. Ryrie *Dispensationalism Revised & Expanded* (Chicago: Moody 2007), 121-122

purposes with salvation. The Dispensationalist, far from confusing these two, or teaching two methods of salvation, *separates* God's plans from His salvation. While salvation by grace alone is always part of God's plan for humanity, there remains the fact that He has in the past, worked uniquely with humanity from one dispensation to the next, as we believe we have shown.

Ryrie continues, "*There are undoubtedly reasons – whether justified or not – why the attack persists. For one thing, the labeling of the present dispensation as that of Grace has been taken to mean that dispensationalism teaches that there was no grace in any other age. Antidispensationalists will not even allow the dispensationalist to speak of less or more grace in various dispensations; it has to be an all or nothing proposition...but the Scriptures declare that even within the confines of a single dispensation God 'gives more [meizon] grace' (James 4:6).*"[15]

Sadly, this is why this book has been written. It would be wonderful if people who disagreed with Dispensationalism actually took the time to think about what theologians like Ryrie are actually stating. Unfortunately, this does not seem to be the case, and their unwillingness (or inability) to do so speaks of a problem that could very well be theirs from the start.

---

[15] Ibid, 122

Chapter 2
Accused and Convicted

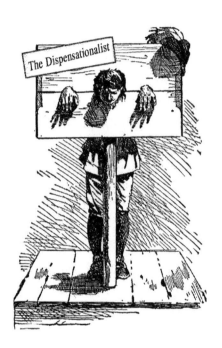

A few months prior to writing this book, I began compiling information and research for reference material. Besides the amount of information I was able to locate, I became dumbfounded when I began to realize just how much venom there is out there for Dispensationalism and Dispensationalists specifically. Some, while at least attempting to be civil, view Dispensationalism as presenting *another* gospel, as I have indicated. Others are far *less* civil, making little to no attempt to hide their condemnation and rancor; using caustic rejoinders and even foul labels in their allusion to Dispensationalists.

I came across another site on the Internet that indicated that Dispensationalists will be among those of whom the Lord says *"Depart from me ye cursed!"* which of course is simply another way of saying that the Dispensationalist is *not* truly saved. This is sad and truly unnecessary, but it speaks of a total lack of understanding on the part of the individuals making these types of statements and corresponding judgments.

This would not bother me as much if there were even a *chance* that they were correct in their demeanor toward Dispensationalism. However, if you have followed the arguments throughout this book so far, it is hoped that you have come to realize that Dispensationalism does *not* teach two methods of salvation, and never has done so.

There is *no one person or group*, which has perfect theological knowledge. It is impossible in this life because we are all at the mercy of the sin nature, in spite of our salvation. No one will get to heaven and learn that what they believed in all areas of theology was the exact truth that God presented.

What is more troubling than anything is the fact that Dispensationalists are summarily dismissed out of hand by many as being heretical. The reasons all stem from those who have *misunderstood* and, based on that misunderstanding, turn around and *misrepresent* what Dispensationalism is said to teach. This is profoundly important to grasp. It is not the fault of Dispensationalism that people mistake it for something that it is not. The fault lies with those who perpetrate a misrepresentation to others, and then those who read or listen to those misrepresentations become satisfied that the truth regarding Dispensationalism has been provided. No further research is done by the hearer.

For many, Dispensationalism is the villain, the modern day liar and cattle rustler. It would appear that there are many who firmly believe that Dispensationalism teaches heresy; therefore, the Dispensationalist is a heretic. Certainly, the Lord cannot be pleased with this type of attitude, which judges another, based on *faulty* reasoning from the start, and the resultant conclusions stemming from that.

I am certainly familiar with Paul's tirade in Galatians against those Judaizers who were trying to draw new Jewish converts to Christianity *back* to Judaism. Through his frustration, he said that he wished they would go all the way and emasculate themselves because of how hard they were pushing *circumcision* as a means of salvation (Galatians 5:12). This is a harsh saying and shows the level of Paul's frustration. Nonetheless, it is doubtful that he really felt that way, but was using hyperbole to emphasize his point. He was very concerned about those he called agitators, who were simply stirring up new Christian converts and attempting to undo what the gospel of Christ had done.

These Judaizers were Jews who had rejected Christ as *the* means of salvation. Since they had rejected Christ, to them there was only *one* viable religion and that was Judaism. As Paul had done prior to his conversion, these Jews were doing. They were literally attempting to overcome Christianity by causing it to *melt* back into Judaism. They felt that Christianity was fine *as long as* the converts continued to practice Judaism. This of course was *not* what Christ came to do, and Paul fought against it in God's power. Judaism was not the end. It was the beginning, which pointed to Christ and His perfect, once-for-all atonement.

Today, the Dispensationalist is often viewed as those who were in some way attempting to corrupt the gospel by adding to it and thereby creating *another* gospel. It is hoped the reader can understand that this stems from the undeniable misrepresentation of *what* the

Dispensationalist believes regarding Christianity and Christ's all-sufficiency.

In my case, I have never believed (nor was I taught), anything except that there has *always* and *only* been one method of salvation. That salvation has always been based on faith in God *through* Christ alone. I was taught this while attending Philadelphia College of Bible (now Philadelphia Biblical University), and more recently while pursuing my Masters in Biblical Studies at Tyndale Theological Seminary, in Texas. Throughout this book, it is my plan to be as exacting as I know how to be. I will take the time to explain how Dispensationalism views not only God's salvation, but also His *sovereignty*, because the two are inextricably bound together.

In our last chapter, we dealt with the various ages, or dispensations that this author believes clearly appear in Scripture. It does not matter what they are called. What matters is that a difference is seen in them from one age to the next, with respect to the level of responsibility and awareness God gave humanity.

Certainly, anyone who would say that the conditions or situation, which existed in the Garden of Eden *prior* to the Fall are the same conditions that existed *after* the Flood, has not carefully read the Bible. The differences are apparent and absolute. However, unlike Covenant Theology, which adheres to a Covenant of Works prior to the Fall, and a Covenant of Grace after the Fall (actually *teaching* two methods of salvation), normal Dispensationalism sees absolutely no difference in the way salvation was received by individuals from one dispensation to the next. We will spend more time on this in a bit.

At no time did any of these different ages have any bearing on the *conditions* for salvation. Salvation has always been, and will always be by *grace*, through faith, in Christ. No works of man are allowed in the equation from the time *before* the Fall to the present day and until eternity, future begins. Nothing man can do will earn salvation.

There is not one thing at any time in human history, past, present or future, which allows man to earn salvation.

Salvation and Dispensationalism

In the last chapter (and reiterated in this one), it was pointed out that despite any differences between the various dispensations, there has been no difference in the method of salvation and how man receives it. There is absolutely *no* difference. It is difficult to say that with more clarity. We will now take the time to go into some depth explaining why that is so.

Many misconceptions exist from those who oppose Dispensationalism. They run the gamut from those who mildly disagree, to those who would like nothing more than to see the "heretical" Dispensationalist dry up and go away. Here is a quote from Bernie L. Gillespie's website, which I believe, sums up the problem concisely:

"One of the first problems of dispensationalism is that it divides salvation - it teaches more than one plan of salvation. Its fatal flaw is the dividing of God's plan, separating His plan for Israel from His plan for the Church...The ages of dispensationalism are taught as temporary stages of salvation. Each dispensation offers a distinct plan or way of salvation. The nature of salvation in each varies according to that particular dispensation. Each dispensation concludes, and the following one is necessitated, by the failure of Mankind to follow its terms, arrangements, or conditions."[16]

First, at no time have I ever *been* taught that salvation is *divided*, or that Dispensationalism teaches more than one plan of salvation. Never. Moreover, I have never read anything by Ryrie, Walvoord, Chafer, or any other noted Dispensationalist that would agree with the above quote. The only possible discrepancy is with the 1909 version of Scofield's Study System Bible and his note on John 1:17,

---

[16] http://www.inchristalone.org/ProblemsDispen.htm

where his poor wording certainly gives rise to the charge that he believed in a grace and works related salvation. In spite of the fact that this was immediately corrected in successive editions, and his entire body of notes and articles in the 1909 edition provide a complete (and correct) view of salvation, those within Covenant Theology continue to point to that misstep.

From the previous chapter, it should be clear that in no way do the Dispensational ages teach different modes or forms of salvation. They simply present additional *responsibilities* and *knowledge*, nothing more and nothing less. You see, the confusion lies solely in the fact that Gillespie's quote is confusing a *dispensation* with *God's plan of salvation*. In other words, as has been stated, when someone who is opposed to Dispensationalism hears the Dispensationalist speak of God's plan, they actually *hear* the words "*God's plan of salvation.*" In truth, the phrase "God's plan" may *not* be delineating, or speaking of His *salvation* at all.

Our friend Mr. Gillespie makes the mistake of automatically equating God's "will" *with* salvation; something that the Dispensationalist does *not* automatically do. Salvation is certainly *part* of God's overall plan, but it is not the *entirety* of that plan. God has many plans and all of those individual plans will culminate together in God's highest purpose at some point in the future.

If we look through the Bible, we can stop anywhere and point to God's will having been accomplished through someone, or some nation. Are we then necessarily speaking of His will with respect to *salvation*? Not always. This turns out to be an unfortunately false accusation that has been leveled against Dispensationalism, based on *faulty* perceptions of God's will and His salvation. These perceptions are simply wrong.

Old Neb
Let us consider Nebuchadnezzar for a moment. We see that God's

will for him was that he would actually lose his mind, lose his kingdom, live like an animal, and then after a time, would be restored. The narrative is included in the first few chapters of the Old Testament book of Daniel. This all happened as recorded, but the question must be asked, why did God do this? It was because Nebuchadnezzar *thought* he was God and God took the time to show him that he was *not*.

Was God's will for Nebuchadnezzar here *equal* to salvation? No. While it is certainly possible that after he was restored, he *did* come around to realizing that he needed God's salvation and certainly the narrative can be taken that way. His attitude toward God had certainly changed by then, which was shown by *what he had come to believe* about God, based on the experience that God put him through. However, what God put Nebuchadnezzar through had nothing directly to do with salvation. God's *plan* was to teach Nebuchadnezzar, finally, that he was not the god he thought he was, and that there was only one true God. God's plan worked.

The Faith of Shadrach, Meshach, and Abednego
How about Shadrach, Meshach, and Abednego, written about in Daniel 3? They went through a harrowing experience under the hand of this very same Nebuchadnezzar. He had made a ruling that stated that every time the *"horn, flute, zither, lyre, harp, pipes and all kinds of music [sounded], [everyone] must fall down and worship the image of gold that King Nebuchadnezzar has set up. Whoever does not fall down and worship will immediately be thrown into a blazing furnace."* This is recorded for us in Daniel 3:5-6. If you valued your life under the rule of Nebuchadnezzar, you obeyed him on this without hesitation.

The trouble was there were at least three young men who did *not* value their lives enough to worry about losing them. They placed a higher value on *believing* God, and proved it by continuing to worship Him just as they had always done.

Of course, we know that this was one of Satan's *plans* to destroy the Jews (and of course, it is understood that none of Satan's plan include salvation). After this rule became law to worship Nebuchadnezzar, it just so happened that some officials of the kingdom came and reported these three young men to Nebuchadnezzar. Gee, what a surprise.

To say that Nebuchadnezzar was hot with anger was an understatement! The text says *"Furious with rage, Nebuchadnezzar summoned Shadrach, Meshach and Abednego. So these men were brought before the king, and Nebuchadnezzar said to them, "Is it true, Shadrach, Meshach and Abednego, that you do not serve my gods or worship the image of gold I have set up?"* (vv. 13-14)

Note their response, showing absolutely no sign of fear: *"O Nebuchadnezzar, we do not need to defend ourselves before you in this matter. If we are thrown into the blazing furnace, the God we serve is able to save us from it, and he will rescue us from your hand, O king. But even if he does not, we want you to know, O king, that we will not serve your gods or worship the image of gold you have set up,"* (Daniel 3:16b-18).

What can be said to that? What absolute grace and faith (and guess Who gave it to them!); what love for God; what absolute dedication to His plans and purposes, not man's. The strength of their faith grew from their *belief* in Him.

Nebuchadnezzar was far from pleased. He pronounced sentence, which was death in the fiery furnace. In fact, he demanded that the furnace be made seven times hotter than normal (cf. verse 19)! While the furnace heated up, it became so hot that the soldiers who tied and dragged the three men toward the furnace *died* from the heat of it! (cf. v. 22)

You undoubtedly know the story, but if not, please read Daniel 3 for yourself. The three men tossed into the inferno, were unscathed by its flames and in fact, it appears that God Himself was with these men in the fire! Moreover, their clothes did not even smell like smoke!

What saved these men? Did their own actions save them? Not at all, because it is clear that they did not necessarily expect to *survive* the fiery furnace. They knew God *could physically* save them, but they gave Him room to choose *not* to do so, which acknowledged and bowed to His sovereignty. Even if they died in that furnace, they knew they would *still* be saved spiritually!

What actually *saved* them was the *believing* attitude they already possessed, with respect to God Himself. They had faith in God and He was the Captain of their fate, fully sovereign. In deferring to His sovereignty, they agreed that God could do with them what He chose to do.

Notice in verses 17 and 18: *"If we are thrown into the blazing furnace, the God we serve is able to save us from it, and he will rescue us from your hand, O king. But even if he does not, we want you to know, O king, that we will not serve your gods or worship the image of gold you have set up."*

It appears without doubt that they already *possessed* salvation. We can see this in their *faith* in God's ability to physically save them (or not), from the fiery furnace, along with their continued dedication to Him regardless of the outcome. Their faith led them *ignore* the dictates of this evil king, Nebuchadnezzar. They were much more interested in pleasing God. They wanted to be men who brought glory to God by bowing to His sovereignty. They knew that faith in Him would accomplish that, regardless of the physical outcome.

This believing attitude *only* exists in someone who already *possesses* salvation. The faith of these three men had allowed them to receive

God's salvation, *long* before the fiery furnace ordeal. Their defiance of Nebuchadnezzar in absolute deference to God was the *outworking* of their existing, inner, saving faith! They could not have had that attitude without the proper faith in God. Being thrown in the furnace did *not* purchase or provide salvation for them! Their faith had allowed them to receive salvation prior to this fiery trial. That same faith enabled them to stand *for* God, *denying* themselves and their lives. Because of faith, they were most willing to take up their cross by dying for Him if that is what He asked them to do, and they were obviously willing to do that with no reservations.

Our Fiery Furnace
The point of this is that in all ages, Christians are required to step up to the plate and stand *for* Christ. No one does this unless his or her faith is *real*. It is only an authentic faith which causes the Christian to *say* what is needed to be said and *do* what is needed to be done, whether the world likes hearing it or not. It is said and done because of the power of the *indwelling* Holy Spirit.

In the end, it does not really matter *what* the world likes. Ultimately, our testimony is about Jesus Christ and it is *Jesus'* reaction we need to be concerned about. He gave up everything for us. Can we do any less?

Shadrach, Meshach, and Abednego believed that God could physically deliver them from the furnace, but might choose not to do so. Each Christian needs to understand that because of our salvation, we also, are called to live a life that exudes evidence of the highest calling: bowing to His sovereignty. This may very well require from us our very lives. No person will be able to give up his life *for* God, unless he has the required faith that accompanies authentic salvation.

Job's Righteousness
How about another Old Testament saint? How about godly Job? Some extremely terrible things happened to Job in the form of the

deaths of many within his household, the loss of herds and crops and finally, injuries to his very person. Things were perpetrated against Job that would cause many of us to die. Yet Job would not curse God, even after his wife urged him to do so. Job would not give in to that sin which would have ultimately dishonored God and brought disgrace on himself.

The book of Job starts out at a run with "*In the land of Uz there lived a man whose name was Job. This man was blameless and upright; he feared God and shunned evil*" (Job 1:1). Interesting.

Job was "blameless and upright." How so? The verse states that he "feared God and shunned evil." Why did he do that? Was it because those actions (fearing and shunning) *made* him blameless and upright, or because his uprightness (another way of saying his *righteousness*), promoted a correct view of God, which prompted the correct pattern of living: fearing Him and shunning evil?

Consider more of the text. We read "*Early in the morning he would sacrifice a burnt offering for each of them, thinking, 'Perhaps my children have sinned and cursed God in their hearts.' This was Job's regular custom*" (Job 1:5b).

Now we are getting to the heart of things. Job was constantly concerned about whether or not he or his children had sinned. He did not want any sin to stand in the way of their relationship with God and he knew it would, if left unconfessed. Job had faith in God. He had faith that God would forgive sin, would heal them if necessary and because of this, Job was essentially a humble man who relied upon God and not himself. He understood that faith pleased God. It was *because* of his faith that he made offerings *to* God. He did *not* offer sacrifices in order to *become* saved, or to *receive* salvation. He offered sacrifices to God *because* he already *had* salvation. To Job, these sacrificial offerings were forms of *worship*, as well as *coverings* for sin (not cancelation of sin).

Even though Job undoubtedly did not fully appreciate the ultimate truth related to these sacrifices (about Christ), he certainly would have understood the importance of the shedding of blood; the giving of an innocent life to cover someone else's sin. He knew that he needed to offer these things with a *correct* belief (as Abel had done). Offering something just to offer it meant nothing (as in Cain).

Job's attitude toward God was governed by his *faith* in God. Let me say that again. *Job's attitude **toward** God was governed by his faith **in** God.* It stemmed from a proper heart attitude and faith, resulting in the correct outward, physical actions. Are you seeing the picture? Salvation is something that God does *for* man, and man through faith in God appropriates it. Not one person in the Old Testament ever earned his salvation (including Adam and Eve). Not one person in the New Testament ever earned his salvation. Not one person today ever earns his salvation. Earning salvation was never, *ever* an option that God included in salvation. Salvation remains something that God Himself fully accomplished and appropriated *for* man.

Some might ask, "*If Job was right in God's eyes, then why did God allow all of those terrible things to happen to Job?*" The simple answer is that Job was *not* perfect. He had things he needed to work on and these came out at the end of the book, with Job realizing that he did not know as much about things as he originally *thought* he did. The other reason that these things occurred (or were at least recorded), is for *our* benefit, so that we can gain understanding from Job's experiences without having to go through them ourselves. It also allows us to obtain a view *behind* the veil that separates this life from the spiritual realm. There are many, many things to learn from the book of Job. Ultimately, God is fully sovereign and He answers to no one. He is not required to explain Himself and sometimes, it is best left there.

Salvation By Any Other Means Is Not Salvation
Lewis Sperry Chafer, Charles Ryrie, C. I. Scofield, and others are often

reviled and ridiculed for their alleged errant beliefs and teachings on salvation. The tragedy though, is that these godly men are the furthest thing from heretics, yet routinely charged as such.

Regarding C. I. Scofield, in the 1909 edition of the Scofield Study Bible, the Dispensations along with all of Scofield's original notes are listed in the margins at the bottom of many pages throughout. The only possibly questionable view that I could find Scofield espousing regarding salvation is found in the notes for John 1:17 (as previously mentioned), in which he states "*As a dispensation, grace begins with the death and resurrection of Christ (Rom. 3. 24-26; 4. 24, 25). The point of testing is no longer* **legal obedience as the condition of salvation**, *but acceptance or rejection of Christ, with good works as a fruit of salvation...*"[17] (emphasis mine)

This particular (and unfortunate) bolded phrase was modified in later editions to reflect the truth of God's Word *and* the actual meaning of Scofield himself. The remainder of the phrase after the bolded section shows what Scofield understood about *works, which* were never part of salvation, but were the fruit *of* salvation. What is interesting about the bolded section is that it is exactly what Covenant Theology teaches regarding the nature of Adam's and Eve's testing, yet it is the Covenant Theologian who yells the loudest about Scofield's apparent *faux pas* here.

It is regrettable that his position was not *clarified* prior to the publication of the 1909 version of his study Bible. It would have been good had he stated his position more clearly regarding obedience within the arena *of* salvation, and *because of* the exercise of faith. As has been shown throughout this book so far, the *reason* people were counted righteous at all had to do with their *attitude* before God, which was the result of their faith in Him and His (spoken) Word.

---

[17] Rev. C. I. Scofield, D.D. *Scofield Study Bible* (New York: Oxford University Press, 1909, 1917), 1115

This right attitude is what enabled God to *credit* their faith as righteousness, looking ahead to the cross of Christ. It was also from this right attitude that the proper obedience *flowed*. Obedience stems from having the right faith, not the other way around. Scofield certainly knew and taught that and it is unfortunate that he failed to enunciate this more plainly in the note he wrote for John 1:17.

His verifiable understanding of salvation is seen at the front of this very same 1909 edition of the Scofield Study Bible. In a short, one-page article he wrote titled "A Panoramic View of the Bible," he states *"(5) From the beginning to end the Bible testifies to* one redemption. *(6) From beginning to end the Bible has* one great theme – *the person and work of the Christ.*"[18] Here, as well as in other portions of his notes, his full understanding of salvation is easily grasped.

Exodus Teaches Redemption
Another area where Scofield's understanding of salvation can be understood is in the book of Exodus. In one of his notes, Scofield states *"Exodus is the book of redemption, and teaches: (1) redemption is wholly of God (Ex. 3. 7, 8; John 3. 16); (2) redemption is through a person (Ex. 2. 2, note; John 3. 16, 17); (3) redemption is by blood (Ex. 12. 13, 23, 27; 1 Pet. 1. 18); (4) redemption is by power (Ex. 6.6; 13, 14; Rom. 8.2. See Isa. 59. 20, note; Rom. 3. 24, note)."*[19]

In spite of the lack of clarity in his note on John 1:17, it certainly appears that as far as Scofield was concerned, salvation – whether in the Old Testament or the New – is *completely* a work of God. This makes it even more unfortunate that he did not fully explain himself in his original note on John 1:17, but it is certainly understandable that in later editions, it *was* corrected based on the entire body of his correct teaching regarding salvation. Unlike what some may think, it

---

[18] Rev. C. I. Scofield, D.D. *Scofield Study Bible* (New York: Oxford University Press, 1909, 1917), v

[19] Rev. C. I. Scofield, D.D. *Scofield Study Bible* (New York: Oxford University Press, 1909, 1917), 88

was *not* corrected to somehow hide Scofield's "real" understanding or belief about salvation. The full body of his notes, taken as a whole, plainly underscores his understanding about salvation. In his view, there is one form of salvation, not two.

Further Evidence of Scofield's Comprehension of Salvation
In another work of Scofield's, referring to the various dispensations, he states *"These periods are marked off in Scripture by some change in God's method of dealing with mankind, or a portion of mankind, in respect of the two questions: of sin, and of man's responsibility. Each of the dispensations may be regarded as a new test of the natural man, and each ends in judgment, marking his utter failure in every dispensation. Five of these dispensations, or periods of time, have been fulfilled; we are living in the sixth, probably toward its close, and have before us the seventh, and last: the millennium."*[20]

One page over brings us to this statement *"It is this manifestation [the central theme of the Bible is Christ] of Jesus Christ, his Person as 'God manifest in the flesh' (1 Tim. 3. 16), his sacrificial death, and his resurrection, which constitute the Gospel. Unto this all preceding Scripture leads, from this all following Scripture proceeds."*[21]

Scofield's understanding of each dispensation is one of a *test* by God. God gave man more *responsibility,* and in each case **man**, not God failed. Salvation however, was *not* dependent upon the works that these additional responsibilities required. That was never the case. The additional works were given to man as added *responsibilities* only, in order to help man keep God's moral law, or in the case of the establishment of the death penalty, to be able to have some type of legal recourse when a man maliciously killed another man. These in

---

[20] http://www.biblebelievers.com/scofield/scofield_rightly02.html
[21] Rev. C. I. Scofield, D.D. *Scofield Study Bible* (New York: Oxford University Press, 1909, 1917), vi

no way created another form of salvation and had nothing to do with it.

Grace Always Part of the Equation
Scofield also speaks about the law and grace, the latter being something that he is constantly castigated regarding. Yet in the same work quoted above, he explains that "*It is not, of course, meant that there was no law before Moses, any more than that there was no grace and truth before Jesus Christ.*"[22] Here, it is obvious that for Scofield, even in the Old Testament, the grace of God was always on display and available to humanity. One wonders though, why these statements never appear to be quoted by those who are *opposed* to Dispensationalism?

Scofield continues, elaborating on what he means by grace. He espoused the following: "*Three errors have troubled the church concerning the right relation of law to grace:*

*1. **Antinomianism**- the denial of all rule over the lives of believers; the affirmation that men are not required to live holy lives because they are saved by God's free grace, 'They profess that they know God; but in works they deny him, being abominable, and disobedient, and unto every good work reprobate' (Titus 1: 16).*

'For there are certain men crept in unawares, who were before of old ordained to this condemnation; ungodly men, turning the grace of our God into lasciviousness, and denying the only Lord God, and our Lord Jesus Christ' (Jude verse 4).

*2. **Ceremonialism**- the demand that believers should observe the Levitical ordinances.* **The modern form of this error is the teaching that Christian ordinances are essential to salvation** *[emphasis added].*

---

[22] http://www.biblebelievers.com/scofield/scofield_rightly06.html

'And certain men which came down from Judaea taught the brethren, and said, Except ye be circumcised after the manner of Moses, ye cannot be saved' (Acts 15:1).

*3. **Galatianism**- the mingling of law and grace; the teaching that justification is partly by grace, partly by law, or, that grace is given to enable an otherwise helpless sinner to keep the law. Against this error, the most wide-spread of all, the solemn warnings, the. unanswerable logic, the emphatic declarations of the Epistle to the Galatians are God's conclusive answer."*[23]

Scofield sees the Gospel message throughout the Old Testament. In one of his notes for the book of Leviticus, regarding the leper and the priest (cf. Lev. 13), he explains *"As a type of Gospel salvation the points are: (1) The leper does **nothing** (Rom. 4. 4, 5); (2) the priest seeks the leper, not the leper the priest (Lk. 19. 10); (3) 'without shedding of blood is no remission' (Heb. 9. 22); (4) 'and if Christ be not raised, your faith is vain' (1 Cor. 15. 17)."*[24] (emphasis added)

So here in the Old Testament, Scofield teaches that salvation came by *no* work of man ("the leper does nothing"), and salvation comes by God *alone* ("the priest seeks the leper"). It certainly seems plain enough that he is repudiating anything that adds to salvation. It bears noting that ALL of the notes I have referenced came from the Scofield Study System Bible, edition 1909, unless otherwise noted.

We will bring cogent points like these from Scofield, Chafer and other Dispensationalists to the forefront throughout this book. Just as in the Bible, it is *impossible* to grasp the meaning of Scripture unless Scripture is allowed to interpret itself, so also should an individual's entire body of work be highlighted in order to grasp his full meaning and intent of what he believes and teaches.

---

[23] http://www.biblebelievers.com/scofield/scofield_rightly06.html
[24] Rev. C. I. Scofield, D.D. *Scofield Study Bible* (New York: Oxford University Press, 1909, 1917), 143

As has been stated, it would appear as though those who are not Dispensationalists, feel compelled to come out against it because they seem to think that a "plan" of God is the same thing as the "salvation" of God. This can be clearly seen in this quote from Bernie L. Gillespie: *"The key distinction of dispensationalism is the teaching that God has two plans at work in salvation history: one for Israel and one for the Church."*[25]

Gillespie then states *"This cannot be understated: the dispensational distinction between Israel and the Church creates serious implications for the nature of the Church and the Gospel itself. Since the Church is considered by dispensationalists to be a "parenthesis" in God's plan for Israel, dispensationalists say the promises to Israel in the Old Testament are not - cannot be - fulfilled in the Church. The Church came about because Israel rejected the Kingdom Christ offered to them."*[26]

However, you see, Gillespie is sadly doing what many people do. He is making a connection between God's *salvation* and His *purposes* for people or nations as if they are the same, when no connection *necessarily or directly* exists. Nowhere does Dispensationalism teach that God had or has two plans of salvation at work in history, yet this is the consistent charge.

Old Pharaoh and Others
If we consider the Pharaoh of Egypt we see that God had a *plan* for Pharaoh. We can observe His plan in the book of Exodus. What was God's *purpose* with Pharaoh? Put simply, it was that Pharaoh would *glorify God* in no uncertain terms.

In fact, *everything* that God does is for the *purpose* of bringing glory to Himself! Certainly, salvation brings Him *much* glory. However, Pharaoh brought Him glory as well and he was *not* saved! Judas brought Him glory! Satan brings Him glory! Everything that exists

---

[25] http://www.inchristalone.org/WhatDispensation.htm
[26] http://www.inchristalone.org/WhatDispensation.htm

ultimately brings glory to God in the highest. Yet many of these individuals were not, nor will ever *be saved*. Pharaoh died in the waters of the Red Sea, along with his army. He did not have God's salvation, yet his life and his death brought glory to God.

Judas died by his own hand, mourning the fact that he had betrayed an innocent Man. Did he have salvation before he died? We know from Scripture and from Christ's own mouth that he did not (cf. Matthew 26:20). Did Judas *glorify* God? Without a doubt. It was due to his transaction with the devil that Christ was betrayed and eventually crucified. That transaction for 30 pieces of silver kicked off the events that wound up fulfilling many portions of Scripture. Did those events glorify God? Absolutely! That was part of His *plan* and those aspects of His plan were *fulfilled*!

What about the coming Antichrist? Certainly, the man who comes on the world's scene at the end of the age will be used by God to accomplish His will, His plan, and His purposes – whatever you would like to call it. However, *nowhere* in Scripture is it stated that God's plan of *salvation* extends to the Antichrist. Satan will never receive salvation, nor the rest of the fallen angels, in spite of what certain religions believe. God will never hold out salvation as an offer to the Antichrist. It is not possible for the Antichrist to receive it.

In this case then, we are able to say that God has plans *for* the Antichrist. God's plans will bring absolute glory to Himself through the Antichrist, as the *only* God of the universe and beyond. The Antichrist will be used of God as an arm of His judgment to the inhabitants of the earth. He will use Antichrist to purify the nation of Israel. He will use Antichrist to bring His salvation to His remnant and multitudes of Gentiles throughout the world, but in absolutely *no* sense will the Antichrist himself, be offered salvation, nor will he be able to receive it. All of this is clearly laid out in the books of Daniel, Ezekiel, Revelation, and numerous others.

God's plan includes *using* the Antichrist for His own special purposes. There are many such instances in the Bible where this is so. One more should suffice.

In the book of Revelation, many events occur under the direct management and supervision of God's *sovereignty*. In fact, it is supremely clear from this book alone that God uses holy *and* unholy angels to do His bidding. This statement from Revelation 9:15 clarifies this: *"And the four angels were loosed, which were prepared for an hour, and a day, and a month, and a year, for to slay the third part of men."* This one such statement in which it is obvious that those angels who are let loose to wreak havoc on earth, were created specifically for that event. The text says that they *"were prepared for an hour, and a day, and a month, and a year."*

In other words, those four angels were created and set aside *for that purpose*; to be let loose at the precise time God had ordained it to be so, in eternity past. There is no evidence that God's salvation was available to them at all. They were made for that specific time and for that specific event.

It should be supremely clear that God has *plans and purposes* that are altogether *separate* from His *plan of salvation*. These two do not necessarily have to be the same thing and in many cases, they are not. While God's plans and purposes can and often do *incorporate* His salvation, this is not always so.

Covenant of Works
What of Covenant Theology and its system? How do they personally view and explain their own covenants? Within Covenant Theology, there are essentially two covenants (though some opt for three): 1) The Covenant of Works, and 2) The Covenant of Grace. What do these covenants mean if not summed up in their own titles? Obviously, the Covenant of Works was just that: *works* done by the individual (in Adam's and Eve's case only), to receive God's favor and His

salvation. We went over this fairly thoroughly already, though it is good to touch on it again.

The Covenant of Grace then is just the opposite: God provides salvation and He alone, with no accompanying works by man needed, or accepted. This is actually no different from the way Dispensationalists understand God's use of His own grace, but for the Dispensationalist, Adam and Eve are also included in this. Grace has been part of every dispensation, for without it, man is completely lost, without hope.

Certainly, this is a very succinct definition of each covenant, yet one can only wonder why there is such furor over the Dispensationalist's system in which one particular period is called the Age or Dispensation of Grace? How is this any different from the Covenant theologian who refers to the present "age" as being governed by the Covenant of Grace? Is it because the age of Grace implies a specific period, but prior to that, grace was not available? That is likely the key, however, we have shown that Scofield knew and understood that grace was available from Genesis to Revelation!

Berkhof defines for us what the Covenant of Works in his Systematic Theology means. He states "*[Adam] was given the promise of eternal life in the way of obedience, and thus by the gracious disposition of God acquired certain conditional rights.* **This covenant enabled Adam to obtain eternal life for himself and for his descendants in the way of obedience.**"[27] (emphasis mine)

Berkhof's statement plainly states that *works* saved Adam and Eve. During the time in the Garden of Eden, prior the Fall, Adam and Eve were placed in the position of having to obtain eternal life through their *obedience*, which of course is an *outward* act. Berkhof says nothing about Adam or Eve's *faith in* God. It is difficult to see how

---

[27] Louis Berkhof, *Systematic Theology* (Grand Rapids: Eerdmans Publishing Co. 1996), 215

salvation was has *not* changed for the Covenant Theologian, because the method of salvation *has* changed in their system.

Covenant Theology clearly teaches that for Adam and Eve, the Covenant of Works was the established way of obtaining eternal life. Had they obeyed God perfectly, eternal life would have been theirs. However, since this turned out not to be the case, eternal life was lost, requiring God to institute another method of salvation: one in which faith was exhibited in Jesus and His propitiation for humanity on Calvary's cross.

Interestingly enough, it turns out that the Covenant Theologian actually believes and teaches what they accuse Dispensationalism of believing and teaching. Yet, in Dispensationalism, salvation has *never* changed. Salvation has *always* been available to humanity (including Adam and Eve) the same way; via *faith* in God's Word.

Again, the different areas of responsibility found within each dispensation have nothing to do with salvation. They have everything to do with determining man's heart attitude toward God, by adding more responsibility and knowledge.

In the Dispensational model, God tested Adam and Eve in the Garden of Eden to determine whether or not they would choose to continue to believe Him, or if they would *shift* their allegiance to Satan. We know of course that they failed the test. They made a deliberate decision to *believe* Satan, and by that choice, called God a liar. This decision to believe Satan caused outward disobedience, but the sin had already taken root within them in the area of disbelief.

In each successive dispensation, the test is essentially the same. God provides responsibilities to humanity in the form of laws and rules (just as He had done in the Garden of Eden), and man is given the choice to *believe* God, or not. To believe Him means continued fellowship and blessing and is evidenced by following God's commands.

Not believing God means loss of fellowship (as a nation), judgment, and in some cases, the death of individuals within the nation of Israel.

Ultimately, it all stems from the heart. It all begins there. The outward *actions* are the *result* of the way the heart *believes*. For the Dispensationalist, there is never any underlying difference from one dispensation to the next. Each dispensation, while indicating unique responsibilities that might not be included in another, has at its root, the same question: *Will man believe God or not?* That question is asked in every dispensation. That is *the* reason for Israel's judgment time after time. It was a resolute refusal to believe God, and this sinful unbelief resulted in sinful external actions, which did nothing but displease God and require His judgment. Since God dealt with Israel as a nation, this is why the *entire* nation suffered the consequences of disbelief and rebellion of *some* within the nation. His fairness and patience allowed Him to deal more specifically with the actual transgressors in many cases, but the nation itself still felt the wrath of His judgment.

The additional information God provided within the confines of each dispensation eventually realized the full progression of His will in all things. From Genesis to Revelation, we have what God has chosen to reveal to us, and we can see that His revelation took place over a period of 1600 years or so, using over 40 human authors. He has shown us the beginning, the middle, and the end.

God has left a good deal out of the record. The reason He has done that is the more we know, the more the enemy knows. It leaves Satan guessing as well. In the end, the additional information, requirements, and responsibilities that God progressively revealed over the course of all the various dispensations, eventually culminate in one ultimate purpose for the reason this earth was created and given to mankind as his home.

Renald Showers sums up an important distinction between the ways the Dispensationalist and the Covenant Theologian view the reason God has done anything: *"Covenant Theology sees the ultimate goal of history as being the glory of God through the redemption of the elect. Although the redemption of elect human beings is a very important part of God's purpose for history, it is only one part of that purpose. During the course of history, God not only has a program for the elect but also a program for the nonelect (Rom. 9:10-23). In addition, God has different programs for nations (Job 12:23; Isa. 14:24-27; Jer. 10:7; Dan. 2:36-45), rulers (Isa. 44:28-45:7; Dan. 4:17), Satan (Jn. 12:31; Rom. 16:20; Rev. 12:7-10; 20:1-3), and nature (Mt. 19:28; Acts 3:19-21; Rom. 8:19-22). Since God has many different programs which He is operating during the course of history, all of them must be contributing something to His ultimate purpose for history. Thus, the ultimate goal of history has to be large enough to incorporate all of God's programs, not just one of them."*[28]

Dr. Showers has hit the nail on the head here. The Covenant Theologian sees God's purpose in salvation as being the *only* purpose He has ever instated. In other words, for them, everything points to salvation. This is precisely why the Covenant Theologian continually confuses this fact when attempting to analyze Dispensationalism. Dispensationalism does *not always* use the terms "God's plan," "God's purpose," "God's will," to mean "God's salvation." The Covenant Theologian on the other hand, *always* sees "God's salvation" as being "God's plan," "God's purpose," or "God's will."

It is this understanding that the Covenant Theologian *brings* to Dispensationalism that actually creates their error. In applying the same understanding to Dispensationalism as they do to Covenant Theology, the confusion occurs because of their *misunderstanding* of what the Dispensationalist means when using the same terms. Unfortunately for the Covenant Theologian (as well as the Dispensational-

---

[28] Renald Showers *There Really Is a Difference!* (Bellmawr: Friends of Israel 2006), 20

ist), they seem unable to recognize their own error. They instead view *Dispensationalism* as espousing the error.

Let me give an example from my own life as a teacher. For a number of years, I taught 6th grade in a section of the city that was highly populated with individuals from Laos: Hmong and Lao. Many of these young people came to this country with no English speaking ability. They spoke their own native tongue and in many cases, depending upon where they came from in Laos, they did not even read or write their own language. Certainly for them, being in the United States and immediately placed into a classroom because of their age was intimidating, to say the least.

Many of us teachers underwent special training so that we would be better equipped to help these new students learn in American schools. It was a time of learning for all of us, actually. While I was doing my level best to teach them reading and writing, they were teaching me about their customs and cultures and there were a number of things that teachers needed to know to avoid offending them.

One such custom was that you never patted students on their heads if they were from Southeast Asia. Because of their religious beliefs, to them, the soul resided in the head. To touch that area was a sign of disrespect. Had we, as teachers not learned that, there would have been problems. We always tried to make all students feel comfortable, and that would include a pat on the back or a high-five, or depending upon the age (if they were young), it would be natural to pat the child on the head. Now we had learned that this was not acceptable.

It was impossible to learn everything about their culture and customs, but we certainly did our best. However, as a teacher, I made one particular (and accidental) *faux pas*, which I will never forget! Fortunately, the students understood that no offense was meant by it and they had been in the country long enough to realize that what I did was simply a common American gesture.

One day in class, one new student from Southeast Asia had been having difficulty with one particular part of the lesson. After quite some time working with him, and helping him through his frustration (and the whole class was pulling for him!), he finally "got it." I was so excited, I started clapping as did the rest of the class. He was on a cloud, smiling from ear to ear. I then took my thumb and index finger and formed a circle, and held it up to him. It is the well-known sign that signals "okay!" or "Great job!" All of a sudden, his eyes got tremendously large, and I heard muffled snickers from various places in the room. Instantly, I knew that something was strange, so I asked, "*What?! What did I do?!*"

One of the students said, "*In Laos, when you use that sign, you are referring to someone as a body part.*" I still did not understand. They then explained it a different way. The imagery of the signal is pretty clear, but as it turns out, I had just signaled to this poor kid that he was a...how should I say it...well, that he was a body part often referenced in our culture as a degrading insult.

Well, as you can imagine, I was mortified and apologized profusely. The kids were fine and we all laughed it off. I made sure to share that info with my principal as well, just in case it came back to her. The point of this story is that while a word or a sign can mean one thing to someone, it might not mean the same thing to another person.

It is no different when discussing Dispensationalism or Covenant Theology. In this particular case, the Covenant Theologian comes to the table with *their* understanding of God's will. For them, it is always connected to *salvation*. This is not the case for Dispensationalism as we have seen. In the end, the Covenant Theologian is mistaken, yet sees the Dispensationalist as having the heretical viewpoint about God's *salvation*. In truth, the Dispensationalist understands

God's salvation just fine, and we understand that salvation is only *one* aspect of all that He does. God has many plans and purposes and all of them will do the same thing: *bring glory to Him and His Name.*

We can see this at work with Berkhof, who attempts to negate Dispensationalism by stating, *"the distinction between the law and the gospel is not the same as that between the Old and the New Testament. Neither is it the same as that which present day Dispensationalists make between the dispensation of the law and the dispensation of the gospel."*[29]

First, normal Dispensationalism *never* labels any of the Dispensations as the "dispensation of the gospel," but it is a good point, which shows how many within Covenant Theology errantly view the Dispensation of Grace. Notice also, that on one hand, Berkhof states unequivocally that salvation for Adam was conditioned upon his *obedience,* which is simply another way of saying he had to *earn* it, by his *work*. On the other hand, he states that this covenant was *nothing* like the Dispensationalist model. He *is* certainly right about that, because the Dispensational model clearly teaches that it is *all grace* throughout the entire Bible, from Genesis to Revelation! Works were never part of the picture (**figure 3**).

Berkhof is admitting that under the Covenant of Works (so named), the way to salvation is through *works*. The other major covenant within the Covenantal system is called the Covenant of Grace (and a third is the Covenant of Redemption).

What seems unusually ironic is how the Covenant Theologian seems not to be bothered by this apparent contradiction. Is eternal life *earned* or is it *awarded*? In Covenant Theology, there is no doubt that at one time, salvation clearly was *earned*. Yet the same folks who es-

---

[29] Louis Berkhof, *Systematic Theology* (Grand Rapids: Eerdmans Publishing Co. 1996), 613

pouse this theology charge that *Dispensationalism* teaches two methods of salvation, when it clearly has not, nor *does* not.

The Bible teaches that we are completely *unable* to help ourselves out of the difficulty which our own sin and sin nature placed us. Free will does *not* help. Yet, Covenant theology teaches that Adam was most certainly able to choose to do right and *obey* God, which would have then given him salvation, or eternal life, based on the outward, *physical act* of obedience. After the fall, under the Covenant of Grace, this same obedience is *no longer* required *for* salvation.

Free Will
One of the most troubling aspects of free will (which is what Adam

Covenant Theology	Dispensationalism
Method of Salvation	**Method of Salvation**

PREFALL: *Covenant of Works*
• Adam/Eve on probation initially
• Required absolute <u>obedience</u> to God
• God promised *eternal life to Adam
• Disobedience resulted in death
• Loss of salvation
	PREFALL: *Innocence*
	• Salvation is by faith in God
	• Adam/Eve required to <u>believe</u> God
	• Disbelief caused disobedience
	• Failure to obey loses blessings
	  • spiritual death (loss of fellowship)
	  • physical death (loss of life)

POSTFALL: *Covenant of Grace*
• All "elect" will repent and believe
• Ability to claim God's promises
• Continually admonished to live according to terms of covenant
	POSTFALL: *Conscience to Millennium*
	• Salvation is by faith in God
	• Man to approach God with a blood sacrifice
	• Before Christ:
	  • Sacrifice pointed <u>forward</u> to the cross of Christ (type of memorial)
	• After Christ:
	  • Lord's Supper looked <u>back</u> to the cross of Christ (type of memorial)

*Covenant Theology states: "God promised eternal life (not natural life) to Adam and his descendants in return for Adam's perfect obedience. Berkhof admits that no such promise is stated in the Bible, but 'the threatened penalty clearly implies such a promise'." (from "There Really Is A Difference!" by Renald Showers, page 10).

and Eve had) is that it seems *always* to be opposed to God's rule; *always*. With the exception of Jesus Christ, there does not appear to be one exception to the rule. Renald Showers refers to this as having *"an unconfirmed favorable disposition toward God,"*[30] because they were not necessarily *pulled* one way or another from within. Please note that Dr. Showers indicates that their disposition toward God was "unconfirmed," but "favorable." In essence, Adam and Eve were truly able to bend either way: to God's will or theirs (motivated by Satan's lie and suggestion). Because of the sin nature that has been passed down from them (after their fall) to everyone (except Jesus), we are *not* in the same position. We are, as Paul says, automatically in a position of enmity toward God (cf. Romans 8:7).

Lucifer, who had free will, ultimately fell due to pride, and became Satan (cf. Isaiah 14:12-14; also 2 Peter 1:19). Adam and Eve, who had free will, fell and died spiritually, and eventually physically.

Covenant Theology	Dispensationalism
God's Highest Purpose	God's Highest Purpose

Redemption:
God's highest, all-encompassing purpose is seen in His plan of *redemption, founded upon the finished work of Christ.
 	
God has <u>one</u> plan, finding its fulfillment in salvation, offered to and received by, the elect of humanity. This plan is designed to glorify Him.
 	
*This view only understands God's plan in terms of His salvation.
	God's Glory:
	God's highest, all-encompassing purpose is seen in His <u>multitude</u> of plans, all of which are designed to bring Him the glory due His Name.
	
	God's many plans include (but are not limited to):
	• Salvation by faith in Christ *alone*
	• His purposes for the nations
	• His purposes for individuals
	• His purposes for those who will <u>never</u> be offered salvation:
	  • Satan
	  • The Fallen Angels
	  • Antichrist
	  • The False Prophet

---

[30] Renald Showers *There Really Is a Difference!* (Bellmawr: Friends of Israel 2006), 33

From their fall, the sin nature, which was created, became an integral part of them, offering a constant, willful resisting force against God's will. There is even indication from Paul that the angels who did *not* fall were the elect angels of God (cf. 1 Timothy 5:21). If they were created the elect angels, they did not have true free will, or their "free" will was such that they only chose to obey *God's* will forever. In essence then, and taking a cue from Dr. Showers, these angels may have had a *confirmed* favorable disposition toward God.

That aside, as far as man is concerned, it appears that even though Adam and Eve had an unconfirmed favorable disposition toward God, the free will that existed within them seemed ultimately *to lean only toward* sin. This is exactly why God is completely *just* in allowing that sin nature, created by the fall, to pass from generation to generation and individual to individual. "*All have sinned and fallen short of God's glory,*" states Paul in Romans chapter three. This is fact. Beings that have free will, seemingly always choose to be their own highest authority; all except Jesus.

It is difficult to assume that Adam even had much of a *chance* to obey God in order to *earn* eternal life. From all indications, free will *always* chooses to go against God. The cards were stacked against Adam in a number of ways because of the apparent nature of free will, which seeks complete autonomous rule, resisting all outside forces. In spite of the fact that both Adam and Eve were in a position that allowed them to be neither necessarily *for* or *against* God's rule, it would appear that free will, by its nature, may very well be too strong for the human being to *control*; certainly a fallen, sinful nature is impossible to manage without Christ.

However, even in this, we see that God had a *plan.* He was certainly not in the heavens wringing His hands, pacing back and forth, bemoaning the fact that Satan was tempting Adam and Eve: "*Oh NO! What am I going to do? Satan is hot on their trail!*" Far from it. What we will see is that this entire situation was part of the *larger* plan having been established by God and which coincided with His *highest purpose* in everything He does (**figure 4**).

Free Will and Jesus
As mentioned, the only exception to this understanding of free will was and is found in the form of Jesus Christ, the God-Man. Fully God and fully Man, Jesus walked through this life with perfect free will intact, never once allowing that free will to give in to a sinful thought or a temptation of any kind. He was, as I was taught at PCB, *able not* to sin, and at the same time, *not able* to sin. Jesus had a perfectly *confirmed favorable disposition* toward the Father.

Imagine taking temptation to its limit and yet never following its dictates, not even once. He never once even *toyed* with the *idea* of succumbing. This is how Jesus lived, as the perfect example of what humanity *was intended* to be from the very beginning, and through faith in Him, *will yet be*.

If there had been *any* chance whatsoever of *any* individual who had ever been born (after Adam and Eve, and aside from Christ) having the ability via free will to choose *for* God, then how would God be *just* in allowing the sin nature to pass along to every person who ever lived (except Christ)? It is obvious then, that man is justifiably guilty and God is righteous and just in allowing the sin nature to pass from person to person throughout all generations. We *all* would have done the exact same thing that Adam and Eve did. Not *one* of us would have done anything different. This is what Paul is teaching in Romans 5:12 when he says, *"Therefore, just as sin came into the world through one man, and death through sin, and so death spread to all men because all sinned."*

It cannot be stated strongly enough that the Covenant of Works and the Covenant of Grace certainly seem to divide God's mercy and grace into two separate compartments that *never* mingle, much more so than anything alleged within Dispensationalism. Yet, the Covenant Theologian does not see this as duplicitous, confusing, or even unbiblical. They see their view as biblical *fact*, in spite of the egregious error within it. The Dispensationalist is given no such benefit of the doubt.

Was It Morally Wrong?
William G. T. Shedd, in his *Dogmatic Theology*, goes even further and breaks down this particular sin by Adam and Eve from all the rest of the sin, which came after it. He says, "*by divine arrangement in the covenant of works, it was only that particular act of disobedience that related to the positive statute given in Eden that was to be probationary. This statute and this transgression alone were to test the obedience of the race. God never gave this commandment a second time. The command not to eat of the tree of knowledge of good and evil would be superfluous after the fall. Fallen man had got the knowledge. Consequently,* **all sins subsequent to this one peculiar transgression of a peculiar statute belonged to a different class from the first sin because they were transgressions of the moral law and the moral law was not the statute chosen by God to decide man's probation**"[31] (emphasis mine).

The above is truly an untenable position to hold, biblically speaking, and I will have to respectfully disagree with Dr. Shedd. The very *root* of Adam and Eve's disobedience *stemmed* from their *lack of continued belief* in God. Is this not one of the sincerest forms of blasphemy, and is this not at the heart of nearly every sin that man commits? Moreover, if left to itself, is not continued *unbelief* to death the only sin that will never be pardoned simply because it is the one sin that keeps individuals from receiving Christ and His salvation?

I agree that Adam and Eve's disobedience was *absolutely* and without doubt the breaking of the *moral* code. It was a moral issue from start

---

[31] William G. T. Shedd, *Dogmatic Theology* (Philipsburg: Reformed Publishing Co. 2003), 479

to finish, and it is wrong to think otherwise. We are not simply talking about their *act of disobedience* though, as if that act occurred in a vacuum, with absolutely no bearing on, or connection to, the moral code of God.

Their outward act of disobedience actually *began* from and *with* man's *moral center*. The Tempter had called God a liar. Adam and Eve *believed* that lie and because of it, sin was born in them. The actual act of disobedience *began* with the thought and belief that God had lied to them. If this does not go to the heart of the moral code, one has to wonder what does.

Since Adam and Eve had determined that God was a liar, the actual act of eating of the forbidden fruit was merely the extension of the sin, which was resident within them. I submit that their sin had already been accomplished when they first decided to *disbelieve* God. This led to the outward act, mirroring the inner attitude.

It Was All for Love
So it appears that Covenant Theology teaches that Adam was put in a position of having to *earn* his salvation. If this is truly what they espouse, it is not what Scripture espouses. In either case, Adam clearly failed and brought condemnation onto the entire human race.

As a Dispensationalist, I contend that Adam was not created to *earn* anything. He was placed in the Garden of Eden along with the other creatures and his wife Eve, to begin something that would ultimately display *God's highest purpose* to the entire universe. God intended to put on display His *absolute sovereignty*, which was seen in His absolute love, justice, and faithfulness. God made the Creation, knowing exactly what would occur *every* step of the way. Nothing took Him by surprise, not one thing.

God *is* infinite. Is He *not* omnipotent and omniscient? If we say that He *is* these things, then how can we possibly state that God did not foresee what would happen with Lucifer, with the one-third of the angels that followed in Lucifer's rebellion, and with Adam's and Eve's willful disobedience? How can we rightly say that God is fully sovereign if we somehow believe that God did not know these things would occur *before* they occurred?

In fact, taken another way, it is accurate to say that God – *being omniscient* – is not only able to see the end from the beginning, but is able to see *all* of the decisions that I have to make throughout my entire life and not mine only, but yours and every other individual that passes through this life. Beyond this though, He sees the results of *every* path I *could* have chosen, even though only one path *is* chosen at each turn. This is incredible if you stop to think about it, but it is certainly in keeping with the nature and character of Eternal God. How could it be any less?

However, God is not merely the *Observer*. He is *intimately* involved in all aspects of my life and plans for my life. Jeremiah 29:11 states: *"For I know the plans I have for you, declares the LORD, plans for welfare and not for evil, to give you a future and a hope."* Of course, we know He is speaking through Jeremiah to the nation of Israel here. He promises them in that verse that His plans are good for them, not meant to bring them harm. Notice that the word "plans" is plural. He has more than one plan for them. It certainly *includes* salvation, but it also includes other things like *prospering* them, *giving* them land, *blessing* them with children, and other things as well.

We can rightly state, that because of Christ, God also has plans for us and His plans *include* salvation of course (which we possess already if we are in Christ), and other things in this life and beyond. His plans for us do not stop once we receive salvation. Moreover, none of His plans are designed to harm us. However, we must be careful here, because if we think merely of the *external* or *physical*, we could wind up coming to the wrong conclusions, which many have already done to their own peril and misappropriation of God's Word. Many Christians have died for God, dying brutal deaths in ages past and even today, in various parts of the world. God obviously does not necessarily mean that His plans are good for us *physically*, although they *could* be (think Shadrach, Meshach, and Abednego). What matters most is in the *spiritual realm,* and this is the point that Christ makes when he states that it is better to lose a hand and go into eternity without it, than to have both hands and go into hell (cf. Matthew 18:8).

God's Plans Are Always Good
God is speaking here of spiritual and eternal blessings. Many Christians down through the centuries have been tortured and even martyred for Christ. Does this *negate* this idea that God only has good things in store for us? Absolutely *not*. Our mind is set on the outward, but God wants us to seek Him in spirit and in truth, from our *inner* being. What is my life that I need to worry about *when* I die or *how* I die? Will I not live eternally with Christ after this life is over? Are not those whose lives were taken from them viciously and often painfully in His Name, with Him now, enjoying the fullness of His presence?

Is it possible that *everything* was designed by God and was done for the ultimate purpose of displaying His love and character to the entire universe, which also highlights His sovereignty by default? Did he conceive everything in order that all He made would witness the perfection of His multi-faceted character and extol His virtues, giving Him the glory that He so richly deserves? Without a doubt, the answer is a resounding, *Yes!*

To the mere mortal, such a display by another mortal would seem not only inappropriate, but also highly egotistical. Yet, this is precisely why God's ways are *not* man's ways. He is so far above us that our puny, finite minds cannot comprehend how someone can so love and yet be so completely devoid of ego! However, God is exactly that.

Salvation Has Not, Nor Does Change

At no time have we indicated or stated that salvation has *changed*, because it has *not*. Salvation is by God's *grace*, through the *faith* of the believer *in* Christ's atoning work, with absolutely nothing added to it. It has *never* been, nor will it *ever* be any different from that. Salvation is *wholly*, *uniquely*, and *completely* a work of God.

It is much the same with the doctrine of election. Either God chose individuals specifically for salvation, or He passed over them. If He *did* elect some and passed over others, then this also attests to His complete sovereignty.

If (as Arminianism states), He did *elect some* based on how *they* would respond to Him, then He is *dependent* upon humanity. This takes away from God's sovereignty and because of that, it should be unequivocally rejected. God is fully sovereign in all that He accomplishes, and salvation is one such area where His sovereignty is fully displayed, as well as His love.

Chapter 3
Progressively Revealed

I remember how I reacted when each of our two children came into this world. When they were born, it was difficult not to start thinking immediately about life *for* them. What would it be like? What would they like in life? What would they *be* like in personality? What would they grow up to be? Would they get through this life without something tragic happening to them? Would they come to receive Jesus as Savior, or reject Him? And so it goes...

Part of the joy of being a parent is watching your children grow up, continually molding them through prayer, modeling, and direct instruction, without overriding their own personalities. All the time we do this, we are watching to see what happens.

I have some interesting memories of my son David, and his particular interests when he was very young. As I have watched him grow, it began to occur to me that he had (and has) some of the same traits that I possess. I had to marvel, because in some ways, it was like seeing a younger version of me. In some ways though, he was certainly his own person. Each of those dispositions came out in interesting ways.

Having played drums for years by listening to records and replicating what I heard, I will be the first to tell you that this is not the best way to learn something, unless of course you happen to be a prodigy. I am *not* a prodigy, but I *am* creative and people tell me that I have talent. Had I learned to play drums the correct way by being taught to read drum charts and learning to play all the para-diddles, I know that I would be much further along than I am now. However, I am fine with that, since drumming is not my career. I have spent many a year playing in this band or that, and I realize that I am not destined to be the best drummer in the world. I simply do not care to be. Drumming is fun and it is also great exercise.

When David was younger, we told him that he had to be in sports or band, which was the same rule we had for our daughter. It was not because we wanted to be difficult as parents. We wanted him to have some outlets that were separate from the computer, which had become and still is, a personal love of his. We wanted him to be well rounded.

He tried getting involved in the school band, even using the same B-flat Cornet that I had used when I was in band in the fifth grade. He tried it and found it wanting; *seriously* wanting. At first, it was actually annoying to hear him practice. This was not because he was necessarily bad at it (though he was, and he would tell you that, too). It was annoying because he was not really *trying*, and having played the instrument myself for years, I knew the difference.

After a while, it actually became a bit funny. He would try to play and wind up just blowing into the mouthpiece with loud unrecognizable tones exiting the bell end of the horn, sounding more like a duck in extreme pain, than a musical instrument. We realized that we were putting a square peg into a round hole.

We suggested sports and he did try that. The problem was that he had asthma, and sometimes it got to the point where we had to run him to the emergency room at midnight. Fortunately, he never died from it, and today I am glad to say that under the watchful care of good doctors, his asthma is well under control.

What were we left with, when all was said and done? If you guessed computers, you are correct. What became terribly difficult for my wife and I was that he could glue himself to a computer like nobody's business! As I write this, he is now nearly 18 years-old and his room looks like the cockpit of the starship *Enterprise*. He has a large color TV, four different gaming consoles, the electric drum set that came with the *Rockband 2*® game and much more to boot!

I personally had given up on him playing a musical instrument, much less my drums, which were set up in the garage. He wanted to know how to play *right now* without having to bother with lessons, or even practicing. That is fine if a person is a musical phenomenon, but like his dad, he was *not*. Yes, it pains me to have to admit that, but it is true.

The Drummer Emerges
It was after we had gotten him the *Rockband* game and he had played it for a while that he came into my office one day and asked, "*Hey Dad, is it all right if I play your drums?*" I was a bit surprised, but said "*Sure, go right ahead. Just make sure the doors and windows are*

closed, all right?" (No point in annoying the neighbors.) He ran downstairs to the garage to see what he could accomplish.

The garage where the drums are kept set up is right below my office, so I could hear them clearly. Frankly, I was not expecting much, or even expecting to hear practicing for any length of time, but I *was* glad he was going to get some exercise!

He began playing – and remember, no lessons – and I began to hear things here and there in the way he was playing, and some of it actually sounded *good*. It was very rough for sure, but there was something there. He played for a while and then quit.

A few days later, he started playing them again, and this time, my jaw dropped to the floor. He started working the double bass pedals into a drum *roll* with the bass drum. I could not believe my ears! I had not taught him that! How had he learned that?!

Over the next few weeks, I noticed some consistency and a determination from him to improve. I gave him some pointers and he started applying them. I also noticed he was doing the same thing I had done when I first started learning: he listened to music through his headphones and simply tried to replicate what he heard. It was remarkable. To date, he is still playing and is even jamming with some of his friends in our garage. They sound pretty good and it is almost like hearing myself, when I was younger!

The Problem of the Spiritual Life
In another area of my son's life, as parents we were much more concerned. It was the area of *spirituality*. Frankly stated, we were not sure if he was a Christian. We knew our daughter was, but with our son, we were thinking that he was *not*. If you are a Christian parent, you know how that feels.

I remember having talks with him, almost pleading with him to receive the Lord. My wife also had a few talks with him as well. Do not get me wrong; we did not beat him over the head with the Bible. We simply explained that without Jesus, there was no hope; either in this life or especially in the next. No one knows when he is going to die, so as long as a person is breathing and aware, he can (and should) receive Jesus.

Time went on, and we continued attending our church. My son would sit there with his arms crossed and with what appeared to be a scowl on his face. I was a bit embarrassed and told our pastor so. He assured me that I should not be worried, but to continue to pray for our son, bring him to church, and let God do His work. Of course, he said he would continue to pray for him as well.

All of this was months ago and I am delighted to share that this past week as I write this, my son followed the Lord in water baptism, of his own volition! The change that is coming over him is noticeable and real and we are eternally grateful to all who prayed for him.

My son's plans for college are to attend a school where he can earn a degree in animation and hopefully, obtain work in that field. He is really gifted there, if I do say so myself. His ability to create something using one of his animation programs, or edit video is remarka-

Secular Plans	Spiritual Plans
Health	Salvation
Happiness	Growth in the Lord
Good education	Good Bible Study Habits
Good job	Solid Church Attendance
Great spouse	Doing the Lord's Will
Happy Family	

ble and he thoroughly enjoys it.

As for our daughter, she is on her way to becoming a Veterinarian, presently in her last year of undergraduate work. Once she graduates, she needs to enter into a specific program and school that provides the type of degree needed to be a Veterinarian. I am literally amazed at what she has been learning: science, math, more science and more math – all the stuff I really do not like at all. She is not crazy about it either, but she pushes herself and does infinitely better than I would do. My wife and I are proud of both our kids, and we are grateful for the way the Lord has been working in their lives to accomplish *His* purposes.

So why did I tell you all of that? Was it just an opportunity to brag about my kids? No, it was an opportunity to point out a couple of things about how the Lord works in and through His children.

Plans and Purposes
This chapter began with essentially a listing of the types of things that parents want for their kids. Most of those things are common to all parents, while some are specific to individual sets of parents.

My wife and I want all the things that I listed. We also wanted to be sure that our kids were *saved*. That is by far, the most important thing that they can receive from God. Everything else pales.

However, if you will notice, not all of those plans that we have for our kids are the same, nor do they all involve salvation.

Figure 5 highlights what I have been talking about so far, with respect to what parents want for their kids. You will notice that I have two columns; one, labeled *secular plans* and the other labeled *spiritual plans*. If we compare the items in each of those lists, it is easy to see why they are separated.

The items under the *secular plans* heading are just that: secular in nature. There is certainly nothing at all wrong with any of them. They are things that most people (not just parents) want to have in life.

The items listed on the *spiritual plans* side highlight items that Christian parents want for their kids. What Christian parent does not want to see their kid(s) in heaven?

However, please notice that the plans I have for my kids on the secular plans side have absolutely *nothing* to do with salvation. God shines the light on the good and bad; the rain on the just and unjust (cf. Matthew 5:45). That list simply represents what most of us consider the good, normal things in life. They are not connected to salvation in such a way that makes me believe that once my kids have salvation, all those things on the secular side will happen.

The items on the right are also plans I have for my kids and it was (and is) to that end that my wife and I spent much time in prayer. We are seeing the Lord answer those prayers.

Would it be fair to say that as parents, my wife and I have two sets of *plans* for our kids? Yes, that would be accurate. Having stated that though, it would be *unfair* and completely *inaccurate* to accuse us of having two separate *methods (or plans) of salvation*, would it not? I cannot imagine anyone accusing us of presenting two different plans of salvation to our kids. If they did, they would simply be wrong.

People in general have all types of plans for their lives, some of which come to fruition and some, which do not. Christians as well have plans for their lives, some of which come to fruition and some, which do not.

God As Parent
As Christians, are we wrong to make plans? Of course not. James makes this clear, but he also tells us that we should submit our plans

to God. He is the one who ultimately determines what takes place in our lives. He is the only Sovereign and His sovereignty over humanity is absolute and complete. His purposes *will* be accomplished whether humanity likes it or not (cf. James 4:13-17).

I would like my son to go to college, earn a degree, and obtain a great job, eventually finding the right wife. Then I would like him to focus on raising a family, which glorifies the Lord. However, what if none of these plans are *God's* plans? What if His plan does *not* include marriage for my son? What if His plan includes marriage, but not kids?

It is fine for Christians to make plans, but it must always be done with the thought in mind that God can (and does at times) override our plans. Why? Because He can, and because He knows what is *best* in all things for us, and because His will and plans for us are the things that glorify Him.

God Chose to Reveal Things Over Time

What I am trying to get folks to realize is that just because the Dispensationalist may teach that God has progressively revealed His will for humanity, this in no way teaches that He has *more* than one plan of salvation.

"This scheme of dispensationalism presents salvation as coming about in a progression."

This comment (written to me in an email), is indicative of the erroneous way people think about Dispensationalism. Notice the terminology used. The person quoted is stating that Dispensationalists believe that salvation came "about in a progression." First, what does *his* comment mean? Does he mean to say that salvation *itself* was merely progressively *revealed* or that salvation has been *progressive*, starting as one thing, and then morphing into something else?

It is apparent that since this individual has a problem with Dispensationalism, he obviously believes that for the Dispensationalist, salvation came to us in *parts*, or in stages, changing as it came to us. This is plainly *untrue* and it is not taught within normative Dispensationalism.

Salvation Has Never Changed
Salvation is salvation is *salvation*. There has only ever been one mode (or plan) of salvation for *every human being*. It was *never* at any point in humanity's history (including Adam's and Eve's), based on *works*. All who become Christians come to salvation through the work of Jesus by faith alone (without works), made possible by God's grace.

The requirement, if you want to call it that, is to *believe* that Jesus Christ came as the God-Man, lived a sinless life, died as the perfect atoning sacrifice for humanity, rose again on the third day, and ascended into heaven. Believing wholeheartedly in this allows God to grant His salvation to that person. Prior to the cross, it was *still* based on believing: believing God's spoken Word.

We are told in numerous places in Scripture that it was Abraham's *faith* that caused God to credit him with righteousness (cf. Genesis 15:6; Romans 4:3; Galatians 3:6). Before Abraham came along, there was Noah and there was Enoch and a few others. Their faith in God is what allowed God to approach them, and He then saw them as righteous, granting them salvation.

God was looking "ahead" to the cross and borrowing against Jesus' righteousness, which stems from it. But remember, the cross is always before Him. Christ's righteousness was then credited to the accounts of Enoch, Noah, Abraham, and many other Old Testament saints.

This is exactly what I was taught at Philadelphia College of Bible, Tyndale Theological Seminary and the church I now attend. More importantly than all of that is this is what the *Bible* teaches.

Salvation is the greatest gift that humanity has ever been in the position to receive. There has never been any work associated with it whatsoever. None. It is a work that God started and completed *by Himself*. All we can do is bow our heads in humble adoration and thanksgiving, and send praises His way. Man does nothing except believe and receive. Even the act or ability to believe is something that God instills within us! It is nothing we do.

When the Dispensationalist states that God has revealed His will or plan *progressively*, it simply means that His will has been revealed in stages. That is all. We are *not* stating that *salvation* itself has *changed* over the thousands of years since God's Creation, but merely aspects of His will and purposes (apart from salvation). It is, however, obvious that as time went on, more *about* salvation became *known* and *understood* by humanity. More will be said on this in a bit. The bottom line is that it was important for God to reveal *only* what He chose to reveal at any given time.

The Germ of an Idea
We can see in Genesis 3 the germ of an idea. The woman's "Seed" would battle it out with Satan's seed. While Satan would bruise the heel of the woman's Seed (Christ), it is clear from the text that Christ would bruise Satan's head, which of course is a *fatal* wound.

That's what we learned about salvation in Genesis 3. That, along with the sacrificial system that God Himself showed Adam and Eve, was all there was to the whole thing at that point in time.

It is extremely easy to see that as time progressed, so also did God's *revelation* regarding what He intended to accomplish in this world. Did either Adam and Eve understand from what God told them that the woman's Seed was Jesus Christ and that He would be born of a virgin, live a sinless life, and then give up His life, shedding His precious blood on Calvary's cross for the world's sin? Even if God *had* decided to tell them that (and there was no need to do so), they would have not understood a word of it. From their perspective, what would a "cross" have been? What is Calvary? What is a virgin and how is one born of a virgin? There was too much information that they did *not* have at their disposal to connect it with the information about the cross work of Christ.

God told them all they needed to know. As time moved onward, God revealed a bit more about that plan. When I say *plan* I am not simply talking about salvation, but it is included. The plan never changed at all. God simply revealed *more* of it, as He needed.

As I also mentioned, it is clear to me that at least one of the reasons God chose to reveal things in stages was because Satan *gained* that same knowledge every time God revealed something new to humanity. Satan knows he will be defeated at some point in the future. He knows that because he *was* defeated at the cross. The actual point in time when his *tangible* defeat takes effect and he is cast into the Lake of Fire has not occurred yet, but it will, and he is aware of it. He does not know *when* it will happen though. He is as much in the dark about his future demise as we are. He can guess though.

Satan is Just as Blind to Aspects of the Future
We do not know when we will die. In fact, we do not know what tomorrow will bring. Satan knows more than we do, but he does not know all of God's plans for the future. He does not know the day or the hour when he will be tossed into the Lake of Fire. He has to wait and see like everyone else.

What possible reason would there have been for God to give us *all* knowledge of the future, so that we would know who the Antichrist will be, when the Rapture will occur, when the exact beginning of the

Tribulation will take place and everything else? Why would God possibly need to inform us of those matters? He does not need to, or He *would*. The only reason we want to know is out of curiosity. We *want* to know because we do *not* know, and we do not like to be kept in the dark.

Studying prophecy is beneficial for any number of reasons. It is fine to understand how it all fits together. In fact, there is really no excuse *not* to understand how it all comes together. But determining *dates* of the Rapture, or the Second Coming, etc., is *ridiculous*. Efforts like that are beyond the scope of human responsibility when it comes to studying prophecy.

Again though, if God were to inform *us*, Satan would then *also* know. Once he knows, then he can plan accordingly. God keeps him guessing by keeping information *from* him.

So without a doubt, God's revealed will has been *progressive* (and this includes full knowledge of salvation), though *salvation* itself has not been progressive. What Abram learned in Genesis 12, 15, and 17, had not been shared with Adam or Eve, Noah, or Enoch, or anyone who came prior to Abraham. No one can intelligently argue that *prior* to Abram, someone knew what God told Abraham in Genesis.

What Daniel was privy to had not been shared with anyone before Daniel. To Daniel was given the interpretations and in at least one case, God told him what the dream was *and* the interpretation so that he could inform Nebuchadnezzar. Daniel is also the only book in the entire Bible, which discusses the 70 weeks of prophecy related to Gentile domination of Israel.

What God told Moses, He had previously told no one else. Prior to Moses, no one made a Tabernacle, an ark of the Covenant, or anything else associated with the rich history of the nation of Israel. No one saw those things because none of it had been revealed to them prior to Moses. Did salvation itself *change* because of those things? *Not one iota*. What was revealed was a greater understanding of what salvation was all about, finding its ultimate fulfillment in Jesus Christ.

There are many things in God's Word that became known only when they were revealed to the people God chose to reveal them to, and *when* He chose to reveal them. This should not at all be difficult for anyone to grasp. This is exactly why they are called *prophets*.

Salvation has always been the same, yet *aspects* of it were revealed over time. I will say that again. Salvation has *always* been the same. Neither Adam nor Eve knew as much *about* salvation, as Moses did, or Isaiah, or Jeremiah, or John the Baptist, or the Apostle Paul, or *you* (if you are a Christian).

Salvation Comes Through Faith: Always Has; Always Will
Salvation has *always* been based on *believing* God. Those who believe that Adam was under some type of covenant or agreement with God are simply *wrong*, and I apologize if that sounds arrogant. It is not meant to be. The truth is that Scripture does not support that idea at all. There was *no* agreement. There was a *rule* that Adam was obliged to follow, given to him by God. Why? Because God created and owned everything. God had (and has) every right to make any rule He wishes.

Before we move along, I would like to look at one individual who shows the clear nature of salvation and the fact that it is based on *faith* alone. Man cannot earn it and has *never* been able to earn it, including Adam and Eve. It has always been by faith.

In the gospel of Luke, we read of a man who was in the last hours of his life. He agonized on the cross, bleeding from the wounds of the nails. The Roman soldiers' whips had shred his back. He was thirsty and in terrible pain. He has no name according to the record of

Scripture, yet he was an extremely valuable person to God. As he hung merely a few feet away from the Author of Life, he initially joined in with the other thief in sending insults and blasphemies Christ's way.

At some point though, a drastic *change* came over this thief. Apparently, he began to see Jesus in a new light. Instead of being angry with Him, he was now finding himself *drawn* to Him. How did this happen? Only by the *sovereignty* of God through the Holy Spirit. This man's eyes had been opened to the truth of who Christ was (and is), as he watched the life in His blood seep from His head, His hands, His back, and His feet.

Can you imagine how large his eyes must have gotten, when the Holy Spirit removed this man's spiritual blindness? He all of a sudden realized that this Jesus, this Christ who hung dying in agony, was a king and not just any king, but *the* King. How could this be? How could this King be nailed to a cross of wood right next to him? After all, as a thief, he was guilty of his crimes and rightfully deserved death (under Roman law), but not this Man. He was different. There was something about Him, which was uniquely uplifting. Yet, He demanded reverence and worship from those who saw Him as He was *then* and is *now*. He drew people to Him and He was now drawing this penitent thief.

By removing the blinders from this thief, the Holy Spirit brought him to the point of being able to say, "*[Lord], remember me when you come into your kingdom*" (Luke 23:42). How do you go from cursing and reviling someone to essentially asking for *salvation*? It happens *only* by God's grace. There is no other way at all.

Jesus knew that the man was being truthful. He knew that this man's heart had changed. He knew that this thief was now *fully* penitent. Think about what the thief was actually asking Jesus.

The thief asked Jesus to *remember* him, and *acknowledged* that Jesus was in fact a king ("*remember me when you come into your kingdom*"). A king always has a kingdom and Jesus was no exception. Though He did not yet have a physical kingdom, the thief had become conscious of the fact that Jesus *would* have it one day. He wanted to be part of that kingdom. He was not looking for anything other than merely to be "remembered" by Jesus. He knew what his life had become. He knew the crimes that had nailed him to his own cross. He was done making excuses for himself. He was literally throwing himself on the mercy of *the* Judge and King.

What he heard from Jesus was far more than he ever hoped he would hear, I am sure: "*Truly, I say to you, today you will be with me in Paradise.*" (Luke 23:43). Is that not incredible? The richness of God's sovereignty, seen in His love, made salvation available to this poor soul on the very day he died, receiving it by faith alone.

The thief exhibited the necessary faith. God opened his eyes and he *believed* that Jesus was *the* King. He was richly rewarded for his faith. He would have had no chance to use any faith at all, unless the Holy Spirit removed his blindness. What more needs to be said? What more *can* be said? God is All in All. His love is infinite and His sovereignty complete. He is worthy to be adored, worthy to be praised, and He is most definitely worthy to be *served*.

Chapter 4
Multi-Faceted

In our last chapter, we discussed the difference between God's plans or purposes apart from salvation, and the tendency of some to confuse *all* of God's plans with salvation. Just as parents have multiple plans for their children, God also has multiple plans for *His* children. More than that though, as we saw even earlier, God has plans for this world and for the nations of the world, and for the people who make up those nations, and for the people who rule over those same nations. Whether they are or are not believers is not the point here. God's sovereignty is over *all* things and His purposes *will* be accomplished.

We saw how He interacted with and ruled over Nebuchadnezzar, Pharaoh, and others. How could anyone read the Bible and determine that God is *not* sovereign; that He is somehow held hostage by humanity? As Paul would say, "May it never be!"

"Because of dispensationalism's aversion to God's sovereignty, and also being predicated on a rigid form of Arminianism (salvation necessary through free will rather than by God's grace), God is viewed as less than almighty or capable of saving the world by himself. This is both a biblical, as well as a supreme theological, error."[32]

I could not disagree with the above quote *more strongly*. I not only disagree with it from a theological perspective, but I disagree with him because he simply does not understand what Dispensationalism espouses, proving it with comments such as these.

The above quote is completely inaccurate and it is so because the person making that statement is seeing Dispensationalism through the eyes of Covenant Theology. This individual wrongly believes that Dispensationalism *segregates* God's plan of salvation for the OT saint, from the NT saint, putting a different set of requirements on each form of salvation presented to each group. Because he makes *that* incorrect assessment, he then extrapolates that, taking it to its natural (but still errant) conclusion, which is that Dispensationalism views God as a *failure*, unable to rule over His own Creation. Unfortunately, what he has also done is build a very nice looking *straw man*, which he has no difficulty knocking down.

The trouble of course is that he *starts* out on the wrong foot, and *continues* on the wrong foot. I hope by now the reader sees that Dispensationalism does *not* doubt God's absolute sovereignty. If this were

---

[32] http://www.inchristalone.org/ProblemsDispen.htm

still in question, then I would humbly ask that you head to back to the beginning of this book and start over, or jot me an email with your question or concern. Better yet, buy a set of Chafer's *Systematic Theology*, or books by Ryrie and set any presuppositions aside.

I am not sure what "rigid Arminianism" actually is, even though he explains it in the parentheses. He says that it is *"salvation [obtained?] through free will rather than by God's grace,"* but I have no idea how he actually got to that point by studying Dispensationalism, though.

It seems possible that he believes that Dispensationalism places more emphasis on man's free will than on God's grace. However, I have already taken the time to explain a bit about free will and that the free will human beings possess now is not the free will that either Adam or Eve possessed. Ours is marred by our sin nature, and even though we are recipients of God's salvation, we are still not free of our marred free will, or for that matter, the sin nature. This will not occur until we find ourselves with Christ. As John says, we will then be as He is (cf. 1 John 3:2). Salvation is *always* by God's grace. Not only that, but *only* those earmarked in eternity past *for* salvation will actually receive salvation.

No More Unadulterated Free Will

We are told in Scripture that man is *unable* choose God (Eph 1:4,5; 2 Tim 1:9; Rom 9:15-18; Titus 3:5, as just a few examples). We choose *ourselves* repeatedly. References like the ones just listed point to a *Total Depravity* in humanity. A definition of this would be: *"The doctrine of total depravity asserts that people are by nature not inclined to love God wholly with heart, mind, and strength, but rather all are inclined to serve their own interests over those of their neighbor and to reject the rule of God."*[33] It is precisely due to this setting of the will *against* choosing God that *God* is required to choose *man*. If He did not choose, no one would be saved. We call this *election*. The Armi-

---
[33] http://en.wikipedia.org/wiki/Total_depravity

nian response to this doctrine is *"conditional election [which] is the belief that God chooses, for eternal salvation, those who He foresees will have faith in Christ. This belief emphasizes the importance of a person's free will."*[34] It is buttressed by the additional doctrine Arminians refer to as *prevenient grace*. *"Prevenient grace is divine grace which precedes human decision."*[35]

Prevenient grace allows people to use their free will (according to this view) in order to *choose* God and His salvation. This view necessitates the understanding that when we speak of God *foreknowing* those who would become heirs of salvation, what is meant is that God looked ahead into the future from eternity past, and *saw* those individuals who *would* be open to receiving His salvation. These He chose *for* salvation. Therefore, in that usage, foreknowledge means simply to know *beforehand*.

However, the actual biblical term means much more than that and in reality includes *appointment*. It also carries with it *"The sense of 'knowing someone beforehand'."*[36] This however, does *not* mean that God only knew who would receive His salvation. The sense is that God deliberately *chose* or *picked out* certain and specific individuals for salvation and for His own purposes. There is nothing within the individual, which attracts God's attention. It is freely by His grace, to whomsoever He will. If rightly understood, this then rules out any form of boasting on our part.

"The apostle Paul points out quite clearly that God has chosen individuals that they might be His people in Christ. He has not chosen them because of any foreseen faith or good works, but simply according to His own holy and sovereign will (Rom. 9-11; Eph. 1:3-12). This choice by God is a selection for salvation. Some would hold that He had cho-

---

[34] http://en.wikipedia.org/wiki/Conditional_election
[35] http://en.wikipedia.org/wiki/Prevenient_grace
[36] Stephen D. Renn, Ed. *Expository Dictionary of Bible Words* (Peabody: Hendrickson Publishers 2005), 405

sen them to receive the offer of salvation, but Paul repeatedly points out that, like the Jews of the OT, all men are in rebellion against God. Therefore, when He chooses men to redemption He actually predestines them to adoption as His children in Jesus Christ (Eph. 1:5)."[37]

Arminianism and Dispensationalism in fact, do *not* go together. Again, the individual previously quoted is completely misinformed, but unfortunately passes his comments off as if they are fact.

Let's be clear here: God is *fully* and *absolutely* 100% *sovereign.* He is *not* sitting in the heavens, wringing His hands, with beads of perspiration running down His forehead. He is not worrying about what He will do with this person or that, or this nation or that. He did not throw up His hands and start sweating when Lucifer was found to have iniquity in him. He did not scratch His head when Adam and Eve fell, wondering where *He* went wrong and what He should do now. Adam's fall did not put God in the position having to go with Plan B. There never *was* a Plan B. There has only *always* been Plan A, which has had (and continues to have) *many* facets to it, all moving to some point in future time when everything will culminate as it was also designed.

Nothing more was ever needed or determined by the Godhead. The three members of the Godhead did not sit there and go, *"Look, what if so and so winds up doing this; what do we do then? That's a toughie."* How ridiculous. Either everything happens by God's design or He is *impotent.* The Bible firmly establishes to the contrary that God is *fully* and *totally* in control over *all* that He has established. Is there a portion of Scripture that we can turn and *not* find His sovereignty in evidence?

God is sovereign over all things, including salvation as it applies to humanity. What has occurred since Creation did so because of His

---

[37] Geoffrey W. Bromiley, Gen. Ed. *International Standard Bible Encyclopedia* (Michigan: Eerdmans Publishing, 1982), 57

determinate plan, which took shape in the eternal council of the Godhead of eternity past. We worship this God! This is the *only* God *worth* worshiping! God is wonderfully sovereign! Amen. Praise His Holy Name.

The Nature of God's Plan
There was only *one plan* in God's purposes, and that *plan* has always been multi-faceted with respect to everything *but* salvation. His plan, in other words, incorporates *many, many individual* pieces, including salvation. The salvation part, though certainly one of the greatest pieces of that plan, is still only *one* piece of the *entire* plan for this universe, this world, and humanity itself.

The most wonderful aspect of salvation is that we never do one thing to *earn* it. We either receive it or we do not, but we are *never* placed in a position of having to *earn* any portion of it. This applies to Adam and Eve, the saints of the Old Testament, as well as those who came after them including us today.

Aspects of God's plan, as shown in **Figure 6**, include a sampling of events and people whom God has used to bring about His purposes and *plan*. We of course see this in His Creation. Did God somehow *not* know that Lucifer would fall? Of course, He knew. While God was disappointed, saddened, and even angered, He was *not* surprised. Of course, He knew Lucifer would eventually become Satan.

God also knew that this very same Satan would begin to try to destroy God's perfect Creation. Was God surprised at the fact that Adam and Eve gave in to the Tempter's suggestion and outright lie? Of *course* not. He was saddened. He was angry. He was *not* however, taken by surprise.

Nothing that has ever taken place in the history of the world – before or after Creation – has taken, or will take God by surprise. If anything *were able* to do that, then He would obviously *not* be all knowing or omnipotent.

When God walked into the Garden of Eden after Adam and Eve had sinned and asked, "*Where are you?*" it was certainly *not* because He no clue as to their whereabouts. It was precisely *because* they were hiding that He wanted them to answer Him, as it was not their normal demeanor to be absent when He visited. He wanted them to face what they had done and realize how their sin affected their relation-

Figure 2

ship with one another, and with *Him*.

Later, when it came time to destroy all creatures except those on the ark with Noah, the text tells us that God "repented" that He had made man (cf. Genesis 6:6). Does that mean He had absolutely *no* clue of what would happen? Did He really wish He had not made man because of how things turned out? By now, you should be saying with me, "Of *course* not!" This figure of speech is for our understanding. God never changes His mind (cf. Numbers 23:19; Ezekiel 24:14; Malachi 3:6; James 1:17).

What about the cross of Christ? Obviously, it did not take God by surprise. It did not take Christ by surprise. It *did* however take Satan by surprise! Had he known what the cross would accomplish for humanity and eventually the physical earth, he would never have incited anyone to crucify Christ (cf. Matthew 16:22).

In fact, it is not hard to see just how often Satan tried to thwart God's plans regarding Christ. He used Herod to try to kill Jesus when He was but a baby (cf. Matthew 2). Satan then tried to offer Jesus temptations that He would not be able to refuse, but He *did* refuse them (cf. Matthew 4). Then Satan tried a new tact. Instead of killing Jesus, Satan tried getting the crowds worked up to make Him a King (cf. John 6:15), thereby circumventing God's plan of having Jesus go through the cross. He tried to distract the King of Kings from even going to Jerusalem to be crucified by giving him large groups of people who needed healing (cf. Luke 9:51). Satan also attempted to incite people to kill Jesus before His time (cf. Luke 4:28-44). Satan is nothing if not persistent. None of Satan's attempts to thwart God's plans worked. Jesus sidestepped every one of them. God has never, nor will ever, be taken by surprise.

When God created the nation of Israel, He did so because it was *part* of His plan. The fact that salvation was going to be extended to Gentiles is not only *clear* from the Old Testament, but from the New Testament as well. What was *not* clear to the Old Testament prophets is that God was going to create the Church. They believed that His salvation would be extended to Gentiles *through* the nation of Israel, in much greater measure in the future.

In the New Testament, we clearly see how God worked in many different ways and every one of these ways amounted to the fulfillment of His *plan* for an individual or group.

Where should we begin with Scripture to prove this point? It quickly becomes clear that beginning with the book of Matthew, God had already arranged things so that John the Baptist would be born prior to Christ. By the time Jesus was ready to enter full time ministry, John had already gone ahead of him announcing His arrival. However, all of this – every event that occurred not only in the Bible but also in human history had been *pre-determined* by the Godhead in eternity past.

Christ's Example and Perfection
Every healing that Jesus did, every miracle and every word (and thought) always perfectly reflected the Father's will for Him. Jesus often said that what He did, He did *not* do of Himself, but by the empowering of the Father. He also often said that He came not to do His own will, but the Father's (Luke 2:49; Luke 11:2; John 5:30; John 18:11; John 18:36; Philippians 2:6-11, and many other portions of Scripture).

It can be said that when He taught all of us to pray, the words *"not my will, but Thine be done,"* found in Luke 11, were perfectly lived out in and through His life. It is unfortunate that so many people read these statements from Jesus and take them to mean that He was not actually God. This is unfortunate because it is completely false. It is clear upon reading the entirety of the New Testament alone, that Christ came in order to show us *how* we were supposed to live before the Father *and* to offer His perfect, sinless life as *the* propitiation for sin.

This is exactly the reason Jesus "lowered Himself" and became human (cf. Phil 2).

Christ's Three-Fold Purpose

As Savior of the world, Christ's purpose was *three-fold*:

- *To be the perfect example for humanity*
- *To be the perfect propitiation for sin*
- *To perfectly glorify the Father in everything He did*

Long before Jesus even *got* to the cross on Calvary, He consistently glorified the Father in *all things*. While His life was being prepared for the cross and He maintained His sinless existence in order to be qualified to be the perfect sacrifice, all of the incidents in Christ's life on a *daily* basis were such that He continually glorified the Father.

You can imagine then, in every way – *whether thought, word or deed* – He never failed to live up to the standard set by the Father! Never did He have a sinful, unwarranted thought. Never did He speak hastily, or with malice. He never got angry without godly reason. Jesus was not only the perfect gentleman at every turn, but always satisfied the righteous demands of the Law, ultimately glorifying God every moment of every day. He always submitted Himself to the Father's sovereign will. This is *exactly* what every Christian is supposed to do - glorify the Father in *every* area of life.

The text in Philippians 2:6-11 states, *"who, although He existed in the form of God, did not regard equality with God a thing to be grasped, but emptied Himself, taking the form of a bond-servant, and being made in the likeness of men.*

"Being found in appearance as a man, He humbled Himself by becoming obedient to the point of death, even death on a cross.

"For this reason also, God highly exalted Him, and bestowed on Him the name which is above every name, so that at the name of Jesus EVERY

KNEE WILL BOW, of those who are in heaven and on earth and under the earth, and that every tongue will confess that Jesus Christ is Lord, to the glory of God the Father."

It is not at all difficult to understand *what* Paul is specifically stating here. As he extols the virtues of Christ and His life, he is telling us that Christ, prior to His incarnation, *was* God (*existed in the form of God*), but was willing to lower Himself by becoming human (*did not regard equality with God a thing to be grasped*). Paul is *not* saying that Jesus decided to stop *striving* to *become* God. Paul is clearly stating that He was *already God* and in fact *had always been* God!

Expanding on This

Kenneth Wuest, in his expanded translation of the New Testament from the Greek language states it this way: *"[This is the mind] which is also in Christ Jesus, who has always been and at present continues to subsist in that mode of being in which He gives outward expression of His essential nature, that of absolute deity, which expression comes from and is truly representative of His inner being [that of absolute deity], and who did not after weighing the facts, consider it a treasure to be clutched and retained at all hazards, this being on an equality with deity [in the expression of the divine essence], but himself He emptied, himself He made void, having taken the outward expression of a bondslave, which expression comes from and is truly representative of His nature [as deity], entering into a new state of existence, that of mankind. And being found to be in outward guise as man, He stooped very low, having become obedient [to God the Father] to the extent of death, even such a death as that upon a cross."*[38]

Whew! That is a lot of verbiage, but sometimes when going from one language to another, a word-for-word translation simply does not cut it. More, in this case, is certainly better for our understanding.

---

[38] Kenneth S. Wuest, *The New Testament: An Expanded Translation* (Grand Rapids: Eerdmans Publishing Co, 2004), 462-463

In Wuest's expanded translation, we can see that Jesus, as God the Son, volunteered to place Himself in a *subservient* position to the Father to become a Man (being born into the human race through the virgin Mary). He felt that becoming a little lower than the angels to be able to ultimately offer salvation to humanity was more important than retaining His *full* manifestation of deity and resultant equality with the Father. Because He was fully God, and through the incarnation, became fully human, He was then in a position to identify fully with humanity as well as deity.

He lived His entire life as an *example* to the rest of humanity that this was supposed to be how each person was created to live his or her life before God. He arrived at the cross, never once having submitted to anything other than the Father's will. Being perfect, He was completely *qualified* to offer Himself as atonement for our sin, and this is what He did.

It is obvious (or should be) that Christ did many things and not all of those things He did were directly connected to the issue of salvation. In fact, it becomes clear from Scripture that Christ's *chief* purpose was to glorify the Father in all things (not just in the area of salvation), by submitting to the Father's sovereignty. We see this unmistakably in Christ's High Priestly prayer of John 17.

Blind to the Church for Good Reason
The prophets of the Old Testament understood that God had a plan. They also understood that God's plan had many facets. It was not merely *one* plan that directed everything to *salvation*. Salvation was, and remains, a *huge* part of that plan. However, there are many other areas within that plan, which God had also set in motion.

The prophets of the Old Testament did *not* see their future with the amount of detail in which we now see it. They only saw what God chose to reveal. While they certainly saw the extension of salvation to those outside Israel, they did *not* see the creation of the Church, which was ultimately revealed by Paul in the New Testament (cf. Ephesians 3:1-11; 6:19; Colossians 4:3; Romans 16:25; see also Ephesians 5:28-32).

God Himself kept them blind to this revelation and once again, the *reason* He did so was to keep *Satan* blind to it as well. Had Satan known that the Church was going to be created, he would have undoubtedly put up as much resistance as possible to *keep* that from happening.

God's plan *involves* salvation, but salvation is *not God's entire* plan. It is difficult to make that any clearer. The entire Bible is replete with one facet of God's plan after another. Israel is one part, and the Church is another part of the entirety of His full plan, just as God's dealing with Saul as the first king of Israel was different from His dealing with David as king of Israel.

These are all essential *parts* of God's plan, but in the case of the Church and Israel, they do *not* represent two separate, distinct, and different forms of *salvation*. Salvation is only by faith in God by His grace, and ultimately through the finished work of Jesus Christ on Calvary's cross.

Because God has chosen to deal with humanity differently during different periods, revealing more information and/or assigning more responsibility, this is in **no** way indicative that the *method* of salvation has changed one iota. God is merely unveiling another facet of the diamond He created before time began.

It is not only unfortunate that Covenant Theology seems unable to recognize this difference, but without doubt, it teaches that Adam's salvation was based solely on his *works*. At the same time, while teaching two methods of salvation, it is alleged that Dispensationalism teaches salvation is by grace and works for one group, and grace alone for another. It is extremely difficult to understand why the incongruence of the Covenant Theology position is not more readily apparent.

Berkhof himself goes so far as to break the Covenant of Grace down into various *dispensations* (his word). They are; 1) the enmity between the serpent and the woman, 2) Noah, 3) Abraham, 4) the Sinaitic Covenant, for the Old Testament and clarifies any distinguishing factors of the what Berkhof calls *"The New Testament Dispensation."*[39]

Covenant Theology builds a seeming artificial system of salvation, based purely on *obedience* where *Adam* is concerned. This is based on the belief that a covenant actually existed and was in force between Adam and God, when in reality, no such covenant existed.

A Positive with a Negative, or Just a Positive

In the so-called covenant that God is said to have made with Adam, we see that God essentially *told* Adam that he should *not* eat of the fruit of the tree of knowledge of good and evil. Doing so would result in death, both physical and spiritual.

Everyone understands that part of it. God stated the facts to Adam. The Covenant Theologian calls this is a Covenant of Works. However, if we look at the definition of a *covenant*, we see that it means *"an agreement, usually formal, between two or more persons to do or not do something specified."*[40]

Here is a basic definition of the Covenant of Works: *"The covenant of works was made in the Garden of Eden between God and Adam who represented all mankind as a federal head. (Romans 5:12-21)* **It promised life for obedience and death for disobedience**. *Adam, and all mankind in Adam, broke the covenant, thus standing condemned. The*

---

[39] Louis Berkhof, *Systematic Theology* (Grand Rapids: Eerdman's Publishing 1996), 290-301

[40] http://dictionary.reference.com/browse/covenant

covenant of works continues to function after the fall as the moral law."[41] (emphasis mine)

Please note the sentence, which has been bolded. The definition states that God promised life for *obedience*. Yet, when the actual text is read, God does not actually promise *anything* in the way of a positive at all. All we have is God essentially saying to Adam, *"if you make the mistake of eating of that fruit on that tree, you will die."* There is *no* promise of life through obedience. In fact, Adam and Eve did not know anything other than they were supposed to:

- Be fruitful, multiply and fill the earth
- Subdue it and have dominion over it

Those were the two statements God made to them regarding their responsibilities on earth. Here is what God said directly to Adam in the Garden of Eden with respect to the tree he was to avoid: *"And the LORD God commanded the man, saying, 'You may surely eat of every tree of the garden, but of the tree of the knowledge of good and evil you shall not eat, for in the day that you eat of it you shall surely die',"* (Genesis 2:16-17).

Nowhere is a promise of life (salvation) stated in *exchange* for obedience to God. Certainly, the warning is clear, along with the consequences that would follow if His warning was ignored. There is no stated "up" side of this supposed covenant. Where is the actual promise of life eternal here?

While we know from the chart comparing Covenant Theology and Dispensationalism concerning salvation a few chapters back, Berkhof states that this reward for obedience is *implicit* in the warning, however we have discussed that earlier in this book. A command or rule, while it might have an implicit reward, does not necessarily make a *covenant*.

---

[41] http://en.wikipedia.org/wiki/Covenant_Theology#Covenant_of_works

Driving within the speed limit means that I will not receive a speeding ticket. Disobeying the law and speeding, running a red light, or blowing by a stop sign as if it did not exist puts me in the position of receiving a ticket if a police officer sees me breaking those laws. This does not represent a covenant though. They represent *laws.* If I do not break these laws, I do not receive a ticket.

With respect to Adam's situation, he had no real way of knowing exactly *what* was in store for him if he continued to believe God, leading to obedience. Certainly, one cannot say dogmatically that he would have been the recipient of eternal life, though this was likely the case. From Adam's point of view, there is no way that he would have been expected to understand that this is what the result would have been had he continued to believe God and not eat of the forbidden fruit.

From *our* perspective, this is what we might be tempted to believe would have been the results of this test, had Adam and Eve passed without falling. For Adam though, I believe it is a real stretch to say with surety that the alleged implicit nature of the alleged covenant would have provided eternal life for Adam and Eve.

For God not to discuss this with Adam, yet to expect Adam to have automatically surmised that God would have provided eternal life upon continued obedience is unrealistic. The "up" side of continuing to believe God, leading to obedience, was not even touched on by God. He did not mention it. Certainly in order for someone to enter into any actual covenant *intelligently*, something as important as the positive rewards (not simply the negative consequences), would have to be discussed and clearly understood before an individual would be expected to agree. That is not asking too much and it is clear that this is what God did every time He entered into a *conditional* covenant with a person or a nation like Israel, throughout the OT.

God never *asked* Adam what he thought about the tree. He never said, "*Adam, if you eat the fruit on that tree, you will die. However, if you manage to steer completely clear of it for 30 days, I will grant you eternal life. What are your thoughts on that?*" God said no such thing. He simply presented Adam with a *rule*; a rule that He had every right to expect Adam to obey. "*Adam, do not break my rule, or you will die.*"

Rules Do Not = Covenants

When I drive my car or motorcycle anywhere, I am *legally bound* by the laws that govern my driving. I am required to obey the speed limit laws, pedestrian laws, passing laws, and essentially all the laws that are in place.

If I break any law related to driving and a police officer sees me break that law, he has every right and duty to pull me over and give me a citation. If the law I have broken is bad enough, I might even have my car impounded, or go to jail!

At the same time, if I drive without fault forever, never receiving a ticket for anything, that same police officer is under no obligation to pull me over and give me a gift certificate for my wonderful driving! There is nothing that is built into *laws* that require this. Laws are made for one thing: to inform people what they should *not* do. This is exactly what God gave to Adam: an enforceable *rule*.

It is clear then that not everything is a covenant. Many things are simply laws, or rules. What God told Adam was one such *rule*. Whether it *implies a positive* is beside the point. The law *itself* merely states a negative: if you do not follow this law, there will be negative consequences. Rules are always enforced with *negative* consequences, never a positive reward. Covenants on the other hand, usually either have a plus *and* minus side, or only a plus side (as in the case of an *unconditional* covenant).

It is simply incorrect to say that God entered into any kind of covenantal agreement with Adam. There was no such covenant. God issued a *rule* to Adam. Adam broke the rule and received the consequences for breaking it. There is no indication in Scripture that Adam *agreed* or *disagreed* with God, and there is no indication that Adam was even given the *opportunity* to agree or disagree with God.

Conditional vs. Unconditional

The Covenant Theologian states that this Covenant of Works that God had with Adam was a *conditional* covenant, yet in Scripture when we see God creating an *actual* conditional covenant with Israel, or simply an individual (such as Abraham, or David), there is *always* a reward and a consequence side to the covenant. When it is conditional, this is *always* the case. When it is *unconditional*, meaning a promise that God simply *makes* to a person or to Israel, it is always solely in the form of a *reward* and it can only be broken by God (who states repeatedly that He will not break His promises). We *never* see God make an unconditional covenant with anyone that is *only* connected to negative consequences.

Yet, Covenant Theology would have us believe that God's supposed Covenant of Works with Adam had *two* sides to it. When we read the Scripture, only one side (referring to the negative consequences) is actually stated to Adam. Even though Berkhof insists that the positive reward was *implied*, this is simply not true, as I believe we have shown.

Noah?

Here is Covenant Theology's definition of the Noahic Covenant: *"The Noahic covenant is found in Genesis 9. Although redemption motifs are prominent as Noah and his family are delivered from the judgment waters, the narrative of the flood plays on the creation motifs of Genesis 1 as de-creation and re-creation. The formal terms of the covenant itself more reflect a reaffirmation of the universal created order, than a particular redemptive promise."*[42]

Now again forgive me, but if we look at the actual text, what we see is a *promise by God* to Noah, which we can say *is,* in this case, an *unconditional* covenant. Why? Three reasons:

1. God *promised* that He would never destroy life on the entire earth via a global flood
2. He gave Noah the sign of His covenantal promise: the rainbow
3. Noah had to do absolutely nothing. God simply told Noah what He (God) was going to do.

Here is the text from Genesis 9:9-13: "*'Behold, I establish my covenant with you and your offspring after you, and with every living creature that is with you, the birds, the livestock, and every beast of the earth with you, as many as came out of the ark; it is for every beast of the earth. I establish my covenant with you, that never again shall all flesh be cut off by the waters of the flood, and never again shall there be a flood to destroy the earth.' And God said 'This is the sign of the covenant that I make between me and you and every living creature that is with you, for all future generations: I have set my bow in the cloud, and it shall be a sign of the covenant between me and the earth'.*"

In this unconditional covenantal promise made by God, He is simply *informing* Noah what He (God) is going to do and not do. Noah is merely *listening*. That is the extent of his participation in this covenant. This is an example of an *unconditional* covenant because absolutely nothing is required of Noah. God does not tell Noah that *if* people start becoming evil as they did prior to the Flood, He is keeping His options open. No, God categorically states that He will *never* destroy all life on the planet with a global flood again. Beyond this,

---

[42] http://en.wikipedia.org/wiki/Covenant_Theology#Noahic_covenant

as a sign of His truthfulness, God tells Noah about the rainbow. Every time this shows up in the sky, it will be a reminder of God's promise.

Do you see how this is *unconditional*? Absolutely nothing was required of Noah. He had no responsibility and neither did anyone *after* Noah. The full responsibility of all the terms of that covenant is all on *God*.

It was largely with *conditional* covenants, of which we see many throughout the Old Testament that God entered into partnered *agreements* with Israel. This was certainly not always the case, as there are a number of extremely important *unconditional* covenants, in which God simply *promised* to do specific things with no responsibility required from the other party (cf. Genesis 12, 15, 17). However, when God's promises were *conditional*, the people:

1. Were told about the *blessing* and the *curse* of being obedient to the covenant
2. Were given a chance to *agree* or *disagree*

In Exodus 20, we read the narrative of Moses on Mt. Sinai with God, as God gave him the commandments that the people were to follow. God's majesty was on display on the mountain, to the point that the people became so afraid they pleaded with Moses to ask God only to speak to him. He then would relay God's message to the people (cf. Exodus 20:18-21).

From Exodus 20 to 24, Moses relays all that God had told him regarding how the people of Israel were to live before their God. Rule after rule, situation after situation was delineated for the people of Israel, with details. The entire process was very ceremonial. There was no way that the people of Israel would *not* be aware of what God required of them, in order for Him to complete His end of the covenantal agreement. In Exodus 24:7b-8, we read the words, *"'All that the LORD has spoken we will do, and we will be obedient'."* And Moses took *the blood and threw it on the people and said, 'Behold the blood of the covenant that the LORD has made with you in accordance with all these words'."*

This is merely one example of the process by which God entered into a conditional covenant with someone, in this case, Israel. All of the specifics of the covenant were clearly spelled out so that the people would know what they were agreeing to before God. Because they *agreed* to it, the covenant was *then* signed, sealed, and delivered to them after Moses threw the blood on the people. In essence, they came under the blood covenant and were *bound* by it.

As with any covenant or legal agreement, if one party fails to complete all of their requirements, the covenant is broken. At this point, the other party can choose to sue the party who broke the covenant, or let it go. In either case, the party that did *not* break the covenant is released from further responsibility related to the covenant.

This is basic legal terminology and understanding. No one would enter into a legal agreement without knowing and fully understanding his or her rights and requirements prior to agreeing to the terms of the covenant. To do so would certainly not be considered an intelligent move. Moreover, in today's world, if there is no evidence that both parties understood that a covenant existed, then legally, *no covenant exists*! Seems to me like Covenant Theologians are trying to pull a legal "fast one" here – because if it is unclear that Adam and Eve knew there was a covenant, then legally, there was not a covenant. Most take the time to read a contract when it relates to any obligations on their part. Some go so far as to have the contract read by their lawyer, and the lawyer can then review the contract with them.

Another example is found in the book of Joshua. In chapter one, Joshua takes over the leadership of Israel after Moses' death. God reminds Joshua all that He accomplished for Israel though Moses. The people were to remember and be strong in their faith to the Lord. In this way, they would continue to be blessed. The people responded that they would obey and follow Joshua's command (cf. Joshua 1: 16-18).

When my wife and I were attempting to buy our first home, we found a situation, which was perfect for us. Since I was not working full-time at that point, we knew the Lord would have to provide a miracle if, in fact, He wanted us to have a home. Because our family was growing, staying where we were was simply not going to work any longer.

During the course of our searching, we found a home we really liked. We thought *"There is no way that we'll be able to afford the down payment."* It was a nice home and the price seemed right. Then we actually said to ourselves, *"What are we doing?! We cannot afford the down payment!"*

God had that covered. He had led us to a homeowner who needed to relocate. They really liked their home, but had to sell quickly. They were willing to take $1,000 down and let us take over payments. What they were offering was what is termed a "simple assumption." In this case, there was no credit check, and nothing else required by the buyer, except $1,000 and a signature on the contract as a promise to pay. While we were making payments on that house, that homeowner would not be able to use his military background for the same type of loan to buy another home. In essence, he was taking all the risk.

It was too good to be true, so to be on the safe side, we took the documents to a realtor friend, and he confirmed that all we were required to do was to put $1,000 down and simply continue making payments. The home would be transferred into our name and we would have our house. In roughly two weeks, we had relocated to our new home; it was that simple. This was as close to an "unconditional" covenant as we could get in secular society!

These are examples of different covenants or contracts that people enter into and as seen, the requirements for each are different. Nowhere does God expect people or nations to enter into a covenant with Him without first understanding what *their* responsibilities and requirements are for that particular covenant.

On those occasions where God simply issues a *directive,* we can be sure that this is *not* a covenant in the true sense of the term. It is simply a command, or directive issued by God, and He has every right to expect that it will be followed.

As previously indicated, this is no different from a parent issuing a directive or certain rules to a child. In such a case, the negative consequences do not even need to be listed, but can be implied, unlike any positive rewards, which would need to be delineated.

In truth then, God could have simply said to Adam, "*Do not eat of the fruit on the Tree of Knowledge of Good and Evil,*" and left it at that. He did not need to provide any specific negative consequences that would have resulted from Adam's failure to obey.

What parent says to their son or daughter as that child is getting ready to head out the door, "*Son, be home by 11:00pm. If you do not return home by that hour, then I will take the keys to your car, and you will be grounded for two weeks*"? Certainly, the parent *may* state something similar to that, but there is no *necessity* to do so. They might just say "*Son, please be home no later than 11:00pm.*" The child would understand that he had better be home by the stated hour, or face the consequences, which would be *implied* if not specifically stated. No rewards would necessarily be implied unless specifically stated, however.

The unfortunate difficulty here is that many who hold to Covenant Theology believe strongly that God entered into a *conditional* covenant with Adam, which is why they term this the Covenant of Works.

Attempting to turn God's directive into a covenant of any kind is sadly without merit.

It All Belongs to God

Where was *any* reference to a covenant of any type, where Adam was concerned? You will not find it because it was not there. Adam did *not* enter into any kind of covenant with God at all. The Garden of Eden, the animals on the land, in the sea and in the air, the plants, trees and even Adam and Eve themselves *all belonged to God*. He was the rightful owner, and as owner, He had every right to make the rules and *did* so. He elaborated the responsibilities and the one rule to Adam.

If God had said to Adam (instead of telling him to avoiding the tree), *"Adam, look around you. You can do anything you want on any part of this earth and in this garden. You can eat anything you like. You can call the animals anything that suits you. Whatever pleases you, that you may do, except one thing. There is only one thing you may not do. You may not hop on only one foot immediately before the dawn. On the day that you do that, you will die,"* it *still* would have been a rule, *not* a covenant.

Yes, it is an absurd rule, but it serves to make the point. God was the owner. The owner makes the rules. The person who "works" for the owner has no say, and Adam was most definitely God's worker in the garden and on the earth, but he did *not* have to work for *salvation*. He merely had to continue believing God.

The Boss is Always Right!

I remember working for a manufacturing company in my younger days. It was during the summer between semesters. You know how it goes: we all need money and money allows us to feel independent.

The job was not bad. It was certainly better than tolerable. The money wasn't bad either. What I had a difficult time with was my boss! He made absolutely *no* sense to me at all! One day, he would have one rule, and then the next day, there would be another rule that contradicted the previous one.

It kept us all jumping and wondering what would come next! We all knew as well that since he was the boss, you did what he said. Failure to comply could easily mean being shown the door. No one wanted that, especially me, since I was only there for a few months anyway. So what was I to do? Follow the rules by simply deciding to do what the boss wanted, whether it made sense to me or not.

All of us live with this, if we are employed. We understand the difficulties at times of pleasing the boss by following all of their many dictates. Often, our job performance is routinely reviewed and given a grade. For the first three months of many jobs, the employer can let a person go for any reason at all. Once that three-month probationary period is passed, it becomes more difficult to let an employee go, but it is still not impossible.

If a person works for a company and passes through their probationary period fine, they become a permanent employee. However, if they decide to do something stupid and against the law, like stealing something from the company, they *will* be fired.

In many ways then, Adam was on probation in his new job. He was given his responsibilities related to the care of the garden and all that was associated with it. He was also given one rule to follow. This comprised Adam's job description. While he undoubtedly took care of the garden and all that it contained, he became sidetracked by the one rule that God gave. This rule to avoid the fruit of that one tree became a preoccupation for him and eventually brought him down. Was God responsible for that? Of course not, anymore than an employer could be blamed for having things on hand that people might be tempted to steal. The full responsibility for any theft resides with the person doing the stealing.

I am certain that Adam probably looked over at the Tree of Knowledge of Good and Evil as God pointed it out to him. It is very likely Adam *eventually* began to wonder what was so bad about that tree, and why it would cause him to *die*.

It is difficult to imagine Adam simply looking at the tree, listening to the Lord, then moving on, never thinking of it again. This was obviously not the case. Think about it for a minute. Here was this beautiful garden, with the wonderful smells of the many different types of fruit available to eat. Yet there in the middle of the garden, was a tree that Adam was supposed to treat as if it did not exist!

We know from Eve's statement that the tree was not ugly. It likely smelled just as good as the other trees. Do you not think they wondered *"What is the deal here?! Why are we not allowed to eat of that particular tree? It just doesn't make sense."*

Apparently, neither of them thought to ask the Lord about it. No one came to Him and said, *"Lord, we are finding that we are thinking about, and discussing that tree too much. You essentially asked us to ignore it and yet, it is beautiful to look at and the fruit looks wonderful and smells just as wonderful! What do we do, Lord?"*

Would not the Lord have provided an answer for them? It is logical to assume that not only would He have had an answer, but also there is a real possibility that at that point they would likely have been rewarded with the *removal* of the temptation (in any number of ways).

In recognizing their need for the Lord, they would have been admitting that they were having difficulties avoiding the tree's fruit. At any point in time, they could have gone to Him and asked for His help, but they chose not to do so.

Adam and Eve were *not* perfect. Even though some translations use this word to describe them, we know that it really means *complete*.

They had everything they needed to make the right decisions, yet they were *innocent*, not having been tested; on probation as it were.

Had they been perfect, they never would have given into the temptation to eat of the forbidden fruit. The fact that they *did* confirms their *imperfection*. Therefore, they needed to rely on His strength to overcome and they did not, instead yielding to the temptation set before them.

Covenant Theology has insurmountable difficulties because it sees covenants where no covenants exist. Beyond this, it teaches that Adam and Eve had to *work* for their salvation. This is the very thing they accuse Dispensationalism of teaching, however we have seen that within Dispensationalism this is not the case at all.

Covenant Theology also does not seem to understand the difference between a *conditional* and *unconditional* covenant as taught in Scripture. These are difficult problems, but it does not end here.

There is one other major problem with Covenant Theology needing discussion. It is by far the most egregious problem with their system and it is one that unfortunately falls short of the most important reason why God does anything. Though we have touched on it, we need to investigate it more thoroughly.

Chapter 5
God's Overarching Purpose

As we have seen, *salvation* is an extremely important part of God's multi-faceted plan. We have also learned that it is not the *only* part of His plan. He has a plan for nations and individuals. He raises up kings and He deposes them, and this is all according to His will and good pleasure.

God's Main Purpose in Everything
All of these plans work together and point to one overarching purpose that undergirds everything God *has* done, *is* doing, or *will* do. What we are stating is that while salvation is an indispensable and

extremely important part of God's plan, there is a *higher* purpose for which God does everything.

This is another one of the areas in which Covenant and Dispensational theologians part ways. The Dispensationalist firmly believes that every time an individual receives salvation, *great glory is brought **to** God*. At the same time, since salvation in and of itself is *not* the highest purpose for anything that God accomplishes, there *must* be something else. That one purpose is far higher than salvation, as wonderful and amazing as salvation is for humanity.

The one overarching purpose in everything God accomplishes is for the purpose of His *sovereignty*, in which He is most glorified. His purpose is *to bring glory to Himself* through His sovereignty. God Himself makes this abundantly clear throughout Scripture, as we will soon see. *Everything will give Him glory*, because everything *will* recognize and confess His absolute sovereignty.

Charles Ryrie also brings this point home in one of his books when he states: *"No dispensationalist minimizes the importance of God's saving purpose in the world. But whether it is God's total purpose or even His principal purpose is open to question. The dispensationalist sees a broader purpose in God's program for the world than salvation, and that purpose is His own glory. For the dispensationalist **the glory of God is the governing principle and overall purpose**, and the soteriological program (salvation program) is one of the principal means employed in bringing to pass the greatest demonstration of His own glory....the unifying principle of covenant theology is, in practice, soteriological. The unifying principle of normative dispensationalism is doxological, or the glory of God."*[43] (emphasis mine)

Ryrie continues, clarifying his comment with *"The covenant theologian, in practice, believes this purpose [the underlying purpose of God*

---

[43] Charles Ryrie, *Dispensationalism* (Moody Press, 1995), 93-94

in the world] to be salvation (although covenant theologians strongly emphasize the glory of God in their theology), and the dispensationalist says the purpose is broader than that; namely the glory of God....To the normative dispensationalist, the soteriological, or saving, program of God is not the only program but one of the means God is using in the total program of glorifying Himself. Scripture is not man-centered because His glory is the center. The Bible itself clearly teaches that salvation, important and wonderful as it is, is not an end in itself but is rather a means to the end of glorifying God (Eph. 1:6,12,14)."[44]

To God's Glory? How?

The question of course that must be asked is this: *how does everything God does bring glory to Himself?*

The answer is simply that when God's sovereignty is seen for what it is, and when everything in all of His creation is truly seen as being *under* His complete control, *this* in turn brings glory to Him. This is why statements by folks who believe that Dispensationalism impugns God's sovereignty are even more confusing. It is also how someone like Pharaoh brings glory to God without his receiving salvation.

God's glory is the overarching purpose for all things, and this is seen day in, and day out, in terms of His *sovereignty*. As absolute ruler of all that He creates, He is without doubt, *the* Sovereign God. Since all things will eventually come under His sovereignty (yet, they are technically under His sovereignty *now*), then all glory *will* be given to God, either willingly or unwillingly, and this ultimately *acknowledges* His sovereignty.

Anything that acknowledges and attests to His sovereignty gives Him glory. Of course, it is best to subscribe *voluntarily* to His sovereignty, because the glory He receives from us is *commendable*.

---

[44] Ibid, 40

So when the Pharaoh of old set himself against God, he was ultimately brought to his knees *before* God. He certainly did not go there *willingly*, but he did go there and this glorified God.

When Satan fell, aside from his sin, everything that Satan has managed to do since then (and in truth, even before then), *brings* God glory. Why? Because Satan's actions and plans are *controlled*, or limited by God and hence, attest to God's *sovereignty*.

Satan has no power to resist or thwart God's plans. He is a *player* in the purposes of the Almighty. Satan cannot resist Him, overcome Him, or go beyond the bounds that God sets for him. All of this brings God glory because this recognizes and esteems His *sovereignty*. Satan is limited by God's sovereignty, and anything he is allowed to do (even if it is seen as wreaking havoc in the world), is allowed by this same sovereignty.

When we fell, through Adam and Eve, God was given glory because it became clear who was (and remains) *sovereign* over all things. Either those who are His true followers accomplish his will voluntarily, or His will is accomplished *involuntarily*. Certainly, God's preference is that all come willingly under the mantle of His sovereignty. Nonetheless, even those who do so *unwillingly* attest to His sovereignty because they wind up performing His will anyway.

Man Centered?
Somehow, the Church has been sidetracked. She has unfortunately concluded that the chief end of man is to *save souls*. Yet the Scriptures teach that the chief end of man is to glorify God and to enjoy Him forever (cf. Isaiah 48:11; 1 Chronicles 16:29; 1 Peter 4:11; 1 Corinthians 6:20; 10:31; Philippians 1:20).

Everything points to God: creation, salvation, good kings, evil dictators, acts of love – everything. God's purposes are met in each of these situations.

However, the church has become a body of believers who are taught and believe that *evangelism* and salvation far exceed anything else. The Church has it wrong, because by doing it this way, we have ceased focusing on God, and instead are focusing on man and man's efforts.

Of course, evangelism is extremely important. However, the most important thing any human being can do is to focus on *God,* and submit our will to Him. By giving up our own preferences for His, we *willingly* glorify Him, because we willingly affirm His absolute sovereignty. From this then, salvation and other important areas of God's plan will fall into their natural place. Christ made this clear repeatedly throughout the Gospels, did He not? In fact, one of His prayers which is often prayed in church begins with the words, *"Our Father, who art in heaven, hallowed by thy Name. Thy kingdom come, Thy will be done, on earth as it is in heaven..."* (cf. Matthew 6:9ff).

Please note that Christ teaches us to pray that *God's* plans and purpose will be accomplished on earth, *as it already is being accomplished in heaven.* This is important to understand. Voluntarily fulfilling God's will is the best way of bringing glory to God.

Letting Light Shine
In one of His most famous sermons, which is often referred to as the Sermon on the Mount (cf. Matthew 5), Jesus spoke of how we can and should glorify God. He pointed out the fact that *if* we take the time to voluntarily glorify God by worshiping, adoring, praising, and seeking His righteousness, etc., then the "light" that is created (by God) as a result of those endeavors will in turn glorify God.

This occurs when the lost around us see that "light" that He creates within us as a testimony to His presence and power within us. Upon seeing this, at the very least they will understand that it is something not created by the individual. Since it was not created by the individual, it could have come from only one source;:*God.* Since it came from God, then people will not be able to help *but* give glory to God. They will marvel. They will be humbled. They will seek Him as God opens their blind eyes to His truth. This is what happened within the thief on the cross.

In the average church today where evangelism or salvation is still even considered, the emphasis is on expanding the membership, but not necessarily through the edification of those already attending. It is thought that by increasing the numbers, more will enter into salvation and thus, the purposes of God will be met. In effect then, the churches of today have become very socially minded.

We see no such argument in Scriptures, and if we turn to the book of Acts, we will see the exact opposite, in fact. It is easy to see that evangelism was an important part of the early church. However, evangelism was the natural *outflow* of the early Christians, who sought, more than anything, to bring glory God.

When Christians turn their attention to glorifying God at all costs, the world cannot help but notice! It is that which brings people to the Lord. Anyone can *talk* about Jesus. Anyone can *evangelize*. Anyone can be taught how to preach a sermon. Anyone can *witness by mouth* about God and salvation. The problem though is that many do this without an inner *life* that backs up their verbal and visible witness.

The church today has it turned around. Our chief concern should be glorifying God, which is accomplished when we humbly come under His sovereignty that already exists. With our eyes firmly fixed on Him, we undertake to learn what His plans and purposes include and in which He wants us to participate. Does it not stand to reason then, that the outcome of that will be a *changed* life; one that truly brings Him glory? If our life is daily placed at His disposal, will this not bring Him glory? Will those around us, many of whom are likely lost in sin, not notice this?

Bringing Glory to God

Glorifying God is the chief end of man. It is *the* reason God created anything and everything. Those who are evil, just as Pharaoh brought glory to the Lord as God's sovereignty was showcased over Pharaoh's life, will glorify God.

Every knee will one day bow before Jesus Christ who is Lord of all. It is this and this alone which brings Him glory because, either willingly or unwillingly, all *will* bow the knee. Will not everything that has breath offer praise to the Lord? Whether it is done voluntarily or not is really beside the point. The fact that all things will glorify Him is

the truth that needs to be recognized and asserted.

In **Figure 7**, we see that *everything* that occurs is somehow designed by God and because of that, He is glorified. The supreme reason for everything that has happened since Creation and will continue to happen until the end of the age, is *for* God's glory because all of it comes under His *sovereignty*. The path in the illustration represents salvation, as determined in the council of the Godhead in eternity past, as part of His overall plan. As God progressively revealed *aspects* of His will over time, which included salvation, please note that salvation itself never changed. We have seen that even with Adam and Eve: the one thing they were supposed to do, but failed to do, was to *believe* God's Word. It is no different today. It is believing in God that results in righteousness. It was that way for Adam and Eve *then* and it is that way for us *now*. We are required to take God at His Word.

The rocks in the image (representing Egypt, or Judas, or Satan, etc.), are there to show that while those events and/or people represented by the rocks are not *on the salvation* path, they nonetheless play an extremely important part in God's overall plan to bring Glory to Himself. They still also fall under the rule of God's sovereignty.

Whether it is the Creation, Lucifer's fall to Satan, the Fall of Adam and Eve, Noah's righteousness, the Flood, Moses' righteousness and leadership, the nation of Israel, any of the prophets, Israel's temporary fall and reinstatement (many times over!), John the Baptist, Herod, Jesus' birth, life, death, and resurrection, the birth of the Church, the persecution by Saul, the conversion of Saul – everything that occurs in history – glorifies God because it all falls under the banner of God's *sovereignty*.

Figure 8 on the next page highlights how all things will bring Him glory, and in so doing, will prove His absolute and unwavering *sove-*

All Facets of God's Plan Prove His Sovereignty

God's Highest Purpose:
To be Glorified through His sovereignty

Eternal Order
Great White Throne
Millennium
Israel's Restoration
Second Coming
Tribulation/Great Tribulation
Rapture
70th Week
Plan of Redemption
Christ
Prophets
Moses ——— Israel
Patriarchs
Ishmael–Abraham–Isaac–Jacob
Tower of Babel
The Flood
Adam & Eve/The Fall
Creation

• Nothing will escape God's sovereignty •

Isaiah 45:23-24 and Philippians 2:9-11

Glory is given to God when it is irrevocably shown that everything He has created comes under His sovereignty. There is NOTHING that will not bring Him this glory. Everything will glorify Him by submitting to His sovereignty ("every knee will bow," cf. Isaiah 45:23-24; Philippians 2:9-11).

reignty. To this end, all of His Creation was made. It is to this end that all of His Creation will arrive, willingly or unwillingly.

Everything *will* glorify God through His sovereignty. This is *why* God began the entire process of Creation to begin with: in order that His infinite love and the unchanging nature of His sovereignty would be on display for all of Creation.

Salvation is God's Work
If we truly believe that salvation is *solely* a work of God, then one has to wonder why some work so hard at it. Why do some churches make every secular effort possible to bring in the lost and make the message of Christ *palatable* to the lost? It is almost as if they doubt God's sovereignty.

There is a church down the road that tries every new gimmick known to man to get people into their building. Once in, they try even harder to *keep* them there. They get them to stay (and consistently open their wallets) by utilizing everything in their bag of tricks.

Whether they have a church "carnival," a men's "car show," a coffee house on their campus, food before and after service, or whatever it may be, the emphasis is on what *they* are doing to "bring in the lost." The problem is that their efforts, essentially created by secular marketing companies, simply highlight man's efforts. Salvation is being "dumbed down" in efforts to create a place where the lost feel *safe* and non-threatened. However, the lost *should* feel a bit threatened, as should believers if they can get to a point where God has become so familiar to them. Familiarity not only breeds contempt, but also it shows how easy it is to take God for granted.

Christians act as if God is unable to save people without *their* involvement in the process. While without doubt, we are *commissioned* to spread the gospel, the focus often turns to the *efforts* and *ways* of getting the lost to step foot in the door of the church building by making the process as painless and superficial as possible.

Then, it must be asked, how does *this approach* glorify the Lord? It is another attempt by man to usurp God, believing that man's ways and abilities are much better than God's. This lie, first uttered in the Garden of Eden continues to this very day. However, God *will* be glorified, because He will show that man's efforts come to *nothing*. Not only will man's ways be proven *not* to compete with God's, but also man's ways will be shown for what they are: an attempt to place man on the throne.

Of course, Jesus gave us the Great Commission (cf. Matthew 28:16-29), and it is our responsibility to obey that directive. We are not to obey it in our own strength, but we are to go in the power of the Holy Spirit. The results of our participation in the Great Commission are solely the responsibility of God Himself. He stoops to allow us the opportunity to participate in the spreading the gospel message, but we can never, ever take credit for anyone who comes to know Him through what we might do or say. Remember the thief? His eyes were opened not by debate, or argument, but by the power of the Holy Spirit. Seeing the truth, he received it, and he received it gladly.

The chart dealing with God's sovereignty, gives but a glimpse of how all things work to *prove* that sovereignty. Salvation is but one part of the entire plan created and implemented by God Himself. His sovereignty stands alone. There is *no one* who will threaten His sovereignty.

Chapter 6
Failure Is Not God's Option

As has been shown, Covenant Theology has a tendency to misrepresent aspects of Dispensationalism, making it appear to be something that it is not. Beyond this, the very reason why God displays His power through all that He has created seems to be misunderstood as well.

The charge against Dispensationalism is seen in this quote, from Bernie L. Gillespie, from his online website: *"[Dispensationalism] impugns the sovereignty of God. It teaches that most all of God's plan(s) to save Mankind failed because it was thwarted by human inability.*

That's why dispensationalism teaches that the Church age was a surprise to the prophets. They did not anticipate that when Israel failed to receive Christ that God would turn to the Gentiles. The truth is, the Old Testament does teach that salvation would come to the Gentiles. And the failure of Israel was not a surprise to God, but on the contrary, totally expected. He anticipated all Humanity to fall short of His glory. That is why He determined to the save the world, both Jew and Gentile, slave and free, male and female, in and through Jesus Christ."[45]

Of course, the tragedy here is that nowhere does Dispensationalism advocate that God has failed...*ever*. Mr. Gillespie makes the same mistake others have made by *assuming* that God's plan *always* equals His salvation. Gillespie also assumes that he is correct in understanding God's *current* dealings with Israel; that God has completely and forever rejected them and in its place, created the Church.

However, Mr. Gillespie's sentiment with respect to God and Israel is also *in*correct, in my opinion. Paul makes this perfectly clear in Romans 9 – 11; something that Covenant Theologians have a very difficult time explaining, without allegorizing. This will be dealt with shortly, in this chapter.

Gillespie further confuses the issue with his lack of understanding regarding the nature of the *Church*, believing as he does that it was actually revealed in the Old Testament. He believes this because, as he points out, the prophets *knew* that the gospel would eventually be extended to the Gentiles.

The truth of the matter though, is actually different from what Mr. Gillespie believes. Paul revealed the "mystery" of the Church in its entirety in the New Testament. Gillespie is taking two completely *different* topics (1. The gospel to the Gentiles, and 2. The Church), and treating them as if they are *the same*; however, he has not *shown*

---

[45] http://www.inchristalone.org/PDFiles/Everlasting.PDF

that they are in fact, one in the same. That is because he cannot do it, since Scripture is clear that only Paul and no one before him revealed any aspect of the Church. We will deal with specific Scripture shortly.

On the plus side, Gillespie *is* correct when he states, "*the Old Testament does teach that salvation would come to the Gentiles.*" Certainly, there is no question about that, nor should there be. It is plain from numerous places in Scripture (cf. Genesis 8:20-21; 14:18; 17:4; 22:18; Leviticus 19:33ff; Jonah 3:1; Genesis 17:4; 22:18; Psalms 2:8; Isaiah 42:1, 6; 49:6; cf. Romans 11:1ff; Ephesians 2:11ff).

However, it is *equally* clear that not one of the Old Testament prophets knew of this entity called the *Church*, nor did they know *how* the Church was designed to work *spiritually*. Paul is the one who claims to be the revealer of that mystery (cf. Ephesians 3:1-6). He makes special mention of the fact that "*This mystery is that the Gentiles are fellow heirs, members of the same body, and partakers of the promise in Christ Jesus through the gospel*" (Ephesians 3:6).

In the Bible verse immediately prior to the one quoted, referring to this same mystery, Paul unequivocally states, "*the mystery of Christ, which was **not made known to the sons of men in other generations** as it has now been revealed to his holy apostles and prophets by the Spirit*" (emphasis added). Here then, we see that Gillespie is in disagreement with Paul. While Paul would agree that the prophets foretold of the *extension* of the gospel to Gentiles, he would unequivocally *disagree* that these same prophets knew of the *Church*. In fact, there is no reason to believe that the prophets understood that the gospel would be offered to Gentiles *outside* of Israel. This was being done then, in a very limited fashion. Since Israel was supposed to be *the* light of the world, it is natural to conclude that these prophets likely thought in terms of a *greater* number of Gentiles coming to salvation *through* and *within* the nation of Israel.

Because of the obvious nature of Paul's claims, it is difficult to understand how Mr. Gillespie (or anyone else for that matter), would arrive at the conclusion that one of the main issues at hand between Covenant Theology and Dispensationalism has to do with the *gospel being extended to the Gentiles*. This is simply not the case in God's sovereign plan. God's plan was always to extend the gospel to Gentiles. Dispensationalism does not dispute that. The *mystery* that Paul reveals goes much deeper than simply the extension of the gospel those outside Israel, in which this new entity, called the Church, would be composed of Jewish and Gentile individuals as fellow heirs.

God's Plan
All Christians believe (or should believe), that God has a specific plan for their lives *after* salvation, which may include missionary service, for instance. Other Christians may believe that God has called them to other areas of ministry. Still others may believe that God is moving them toward a specific Christian college, and others feel that God wants them to obtain their education through a secular college.

The unique, individual *plans* God has *for* these Christians do *not* mean that His plan of *salvation* varies from individual to individual. Covenant Theology seems hopelessly lost in the confusion which it alone created by *limiting* God's *plan* to only include salvation.

It is also remarkable that Mr. Gillespie admits that Israel *failed*. Mr. Gillespie might say that God saw ahead and *knew* (I would say *predetermined*) that Israel would fail. It was *because* of this failure that God (in eternity past) extended the gospel to the Gentiles, in order to create the Church.

In truth though, what Dispensationalism actually teaches is that God has a unique plan for *Israel* (within the confines and blessings of salvation, which comes solely by faith) and a unique plan for the *Church* (within the confines and blessings of salvation, which comes solely by faith). Please note that it was not stated that these individual unique plans of God for each group *incorporated only salvation.* Each unique plan, which God instituted for each body (the nation of Israel and the Church), differed in all areas *except* salvation.

It seems clear though, that Gillespie unfortunately believes that Dispensationalism espouses the idea that God has a unique plan of salvation *for* Israel and a different plan of salvation *for* the Church. While this is what it *appears* Mr. Gillespie (as well as many others within Covenant Theology) *hears,* it is most certainly *not* what Dispensationalism teaches, promotes, or seeks to establish.

The Same Salvation
In this particular age, as in all ages past, salvation is the same for the Jew and Gentile. It should be clear at this point, from all that has been stated in this book. Individual, respective Jewish and Gentile standings before God are based *solely* on *faith* in Him. There is no other way in which Jews or Gentiles come to receive salvation and this is clear from Adam and Eve onward. Any works involved are works that are accomplished *after salvation is received,* and *while* the individual is a believer.

Though the salvation is the same for everyone - whether Jew or Gentile - it does *not* automatically follow that God is required to have the same will or purposes *in all areas for both groups.* So then, one must ask why Covenant Theology causes its adherents to come to this *incorrect* conclusion. It must be because many who hold to the tenets of Covenant Theology think of God's *plan* only in terms of *salvation,* in spite of any evidence to the contrary, as has been stated.

It is truly unfortunate that the big picture seems to be continually missed by these good folks, who are obviously earnest in their love for God. Ryrie brings this point to the fore, and is it worth repeating here: *"To the normative dispensationalist, the soteriological, or saving,* *program of God **is not the only program but one of** the means God is using in the total program of glorifying Himself,"*[46] (emphasis added).

My understanding of Scripture is such that God is *fully* sovereign *over all,* whether it actually appears to be the case or not from our vantage point. Where can one go in Scripture and read that God has *ever* failed? It cannot be found, because it is *not* there. God is sovereign, *period,* and there has never been any threat to His sovereignty, nor will there be. He could not be all-powerful, or all knowing if that was even a remote possibility.

Salvation is, as Ryrie says, not an end unto itself, but one of the *means* by which all things will glorify God. As we discussed, *everything* will glorify God, from Adam to Noah, to Pharaoh, to Moses, to the New Testament saints, to you and me. Everything and everyone *will* bring glory to God and *that*, my friends, is the highest purpose of God because it attests to His absolute sovereignty. There is no other purpose that far-reaching. It is all for God's glory and His glory is found in His absolute sovereignty.

Far from "impugning" God's salvation, as Gillespie and others charge, Dispensationalism sees God's sovereignty as *the* absolute highest reason under which *all* His plans and purposes merge, and to which all glory and honor is directed. Every work He has ever undertaken, including salvation, serves to call attention to His *sovereignty*.

The crux of the matter is found in Covenant Theology's inability to see anything except salvation as God's highest purpose. Everything for Covenant Theology in Scripture then comes back to that one doctrine: *salvation*. This is why Dispensationalism is seen as teaching that God failed, though this is not what it teaches. As long as the Covenant Theologian remains unable to see God's *highest purpose* for everything He has done and will do as directing everything to His *so-*

---

[46] Charles Ryrie, *Dispensationalism* (Moody Press, 1995), 40

vereignty, this point will be continually missed. Salvation is *not* the end. It is *one* of the vehicles, which God has chosen to bring glory to Himself.

If we *stop* at salvation, never seeing any reason for God's purposes *beyond* it, we will *fail to see* that *everything* is designed to bring God the glory: Creation, Satan, Pharaoh, the Flood, Moses, Israel, the wilderness wanderings, the Bronze Serpent, Joshua, the cross of Christ, Judas – *all of it!* Everything that exists and takes place, from the Creation (as far as humanity is concerned) until the end of time, and into the beginning of the future eternal order and beyond *will* bring God glory. How is it that Dispensationalism is somehow impugning God's sovereignty?

Has God's Plan(s) Failed?

Dispensationalism does *not* teach that God failed at any time. Proof of that is the fact that normative Dispensationalism teaches that God simply has *unfinished* business with Israel. His ultimate purposes for them have not yet been fulfilled, but *will* be. If God is not done with Israel, how could it possibly be said that He failed in an way, shape, or form? He has not done so.

In reality, it is Covenant Theology, which points to God's alleged failure, with respect to Israel. Let us look closely at what Mr. Gillespie has stated. He alleges that because Dispensationalism simply makes a distinction between Israel and the Church as two separate entities, this somehow provides evidence that the Dispensationalist believes that God has failed. This is predicated on:

1. The belief that Dispensationalism teaches that the Old Testament prophets did not see that the gospel would be extended to Gentiles. (Covenant Theology says that the OT prophets did understand the gospel was to be extended to the Gentiles, therefore the concept of the Church *is* taught in the OT, with full revelation made by Paul in the New Testament.)

2. The belief that salvation was *different* in the Old Testament scheme, from the New Testament scheme. This is in spite of the clarifications made by Scofield, Chafer, Walvoord, Ryrie and others over the years.

First, I know of *no normative* Dispensationalist who believes that salvation was *never* intended to be offered to the Gentiles. Again, Mr. Gillespie lumps two things together, which creates his error (because they are not the same). He believes:

1. **The fact that the OT teaches the gospel would extend to the Gentiles, and**
2. **These OT references actually reveal the Church**

Secondly, notice what our friend, Mr. Gillespie has done. He is *implying* that since the prophets *knew* the gospel would eventually be extended to Gentiles, they actually *did* see the Church. Yet, according to Paul in the Ephesians 3 passage we referenced, these same prophets did *not* see the Church. It was a complete mystery to them!

Mr. Gillespie's error then, stems from the fact that he is equating the extension of the gospel to Gentiles *as* the Church, which further muddies the water, because it is wrong. While the prophets knew of the former, they were completely *unaware* of the latter. The only way to state that the prophets knew of the *Church* is to somehow claim that Paul meant something *else* when he spoke of the "mystery of Christ." However, Paul's words *are* plain enough. God took the Jewish individual and the Gentile individual and from the two, made *one* man out of the two, incorporating both into the *one Body*, which is Christ's Bride. This was *nowhere* seen or testified to by the Old Testament prophets.

There is no difficulty understanding that the Old Testament witnessed to the fact that *through* Abraham all the families of the earth would be blessed (cf. Genesis 12:1-3). That the gospel would include Gentile nations is more than implicit in God's promise to Abraham. Yet, there is no mention of a *Church* (or the mystery of how God would take Jew and Gentile and create *one* man, as explained by Paul in Ephesians 3) in that promise or any other promise that God reiterated either to Abraham, or to any of his descendants throughout the Old Testament. The Old Testament merely teaches that the gospel was to be *extended* to the Gentiles, *not* that the *Church* was to be created.

The Mystery
Paul also alludes to this mystery in the eleventh chapter of Romans, where he is discussing the reason why God went to the Gentiles. He states: *"Lest you be wise in your own sight, I want you to understand this mystery, brothers: a partial hardening has come upon Israel, until the fullness of the Gentiles has come in"* (Romans 11:25). Paul expands on this a bit later on in Romans 16:25-26, and elsewhere. What he is saying is quite clear.

The mystery here is that *while* the gospel is being fully offered to the Gentiles, Israel (as a nation) has been given a partial hardening. While *individual* Jews would become part of the Church, the nation as a whole was set aside in order that God could invite Gentiles to faith through Christ's completed work. This is exactly what God did previously, after He had dealt with their rebellion long enough. He set them aside, *temporarily*.

There are a number of things Paul refers to as *mysteries*. A mystery is something that has not been shared or known *before*. Fruchtenbaum explains, *"In New Testament Greek, the meaning [of 'mystery'] is both technical and simple: It refers to something that was totally* **unrevealed** *in the Old Testament, and only revealed in the New Testa-*

ment"[47] (emphasis added). Specifically here, Paul explains the mystery of Israel's blindness, or partial hardening. The entire mystery is fully detailed in Romans 9-11.

Paul begins in chapter nine by explaining how sorrowful he is; sorrowful to the point of experiencing physical pain over Israel's current lost condition. He highlights the many things that Israel enjoyed, which went with the privileges of being a chosen people.

Paul then moves on to discuss the fact that Israel *rejected* the Messiah (Romans 9:6-13). It is here where people become confused. Let us look at the text.

"But it is not as though the word of God has failed. For not all who are descended from Israel belong to Israel, and not all are children of Abraham because they are his offspring, but 'Through Isaac shall your offspring be named.' This means that it is not the children of the flesh who are the children of God, but the children of the promise are counted as offspring. For this is what the promise said: 'About this time next year I will return, and Sarah shall have a son.' And not only so, but also when Rebekah had conceived children by one man, our forefather Isaac, though they were not yet born and had done nothing either good or bad—in order that God's purpose of election might continue, not because of works but because of him who calls— she was told, 'The older will serve the younger.' As it is written, 'Jacob I loved, but Esau I hated'."

Paul begins by actually referring to the fact that there are *two* Israels. There is *"Israel the whole, including all Jews, all the descendants of Abraham, Isaac and Jacob; then there is the Remnant of Israel, that mi-*

---

[47] Arnold G. Fruchtenbaum, *Footsteps of the Messiah* (San Antonio: Ariel Ministries 2003), 651

nority segment of the Jewish population who are believers."[48] Paul clarifies his comments by comparing each group with Isaac and Ishmael, and Esau and Jacob. He winds up making four points here (as outlined by Fruchtenbaum):

- *"although Israel failed, God's Word has not and, in fact, all is going according to God's plan*
- *"spiritual blessings **do not come** on the basis of **physical** descent or personal merit, but **only to those physical descendants who believe** – and only those physical descendants who believe are Abraham's real spiritual children*
- *"the spiritual blessings come by the grace of God solely through the will of God*
- *"physical descent alone will not obtain these promises, only physical descent and its spiritual appropriation will obtain them, **meaning one must be both physically and spiritually Jewish***

*"To conclude this section, **Paul is not saying that the Church has replaced Israel**. Rather, **his point is that the Remnant of Israel has obtained these promises, while the rest of Israel has no**,"*[49] (emphasis added).

When one takes the time to thoroughly read the text, keeping it *within* its context, Paul's meaning becomes clear. First, he is *speaking* to Jews at this point in Romans, *not to* Gentiles. Since he is speaking to Jewish people, the message should be understood within the confines of that culture. Therefore, Paul states (to Jews) not everyone who came from Abraham is Jewish. He then compares Ishmael to Isaac. While both *came from Abraham's loins*, only one son is the promised son. Both children though, are *physical* descendants of Abraham.

---

[48] Arnold G. Fruchtenbaum, *Footsteps of the Messiah* (San Antonio: Ariel Ministries 2003), 678
[49] Ibid, 678-679

Paul's meaning is that in spite of the fact that Abraham has many physical descendants (through Isaac, and then Jacob, from whom the entire Jewish nation came into being), not *all* of those *physically* Jewish individuals who made up the nation of Israel *received* God's *spiritual* blessings. In fact, many of them died in the wilderness due to judgment by God *because* of their unbelief (which had led to rebellious living before God). This was *while* they were part of the nation of Israel.

It needs to be clearly understood that Paul is not speaking to Gentiles at this point in Romans. He is dealing with his own people, who are Jewish.

Yet it is very common for many Christians to read this section of Romans and say, "*Wow, Christians are spiritual Jews!*" No, Christians are *not* spiritual Jews. We are Gentile Christians *only*. That is *it*; we will *never* be Jewish, either physically or spiritually.

Paul is *not* somehow negating his or anyone else's *physical* Jewish ancestry. He *is* however, clearly pointing out that just because a person is Jewish does not mean that they will automatically obtain salvation . There have been, are now, and will be many Jewish individuals who have not and will *not* receive the promises that God made to Abraham. Only those physical Jews who receive salvation through Christ become *spiritual* Jews. These Jews will receive the promises God made to Abraham at some point in the future.

Israel's Rejection and Consolation
Paul unmistakably teaches here also that Israel's rejection of the Messiah did *not* take God by surprise. We need to ask ourselves: how could Israel's rejection have taken God by surprise if that same rejection was already *prophesied* in the Old Testament in numerous plac-

es, like Isaiah 8:14; 28:16; Psalm 22; 118:22; 52-53, as well as other passages too numerous to list? It neither took God by surprise, nor caused Him to fail.

Later on in Romans 9:30-33, Paul explains the reason for Israel's rejection. He speaks of the fact that Gentiles received what Jews did not because the Gentiles had *faith* in God. The Jews who obviously rejected Christ did *not* have faith in God. Paul also indicates that he is very aware of Jewish zeal for God, but unfortunately, it is not zeal according to *knowledge*. Since they completely misunderstood the actual purpose of the Law, they could not understand their own need to repent and *receive* salvation. They thought the Law already *provided* that, so they were safe! This is the exact same situation, which exists with orthodox or Talmudic Jews today. They believe they can rely on the Law of Moses for their salvation.

Eventually, Paul gets to Romans chapter eleven, where he speaks of Israel's consolation. He clearly indicates in verses 1-10 that Israel's rejection of the Messiah was *not total*, meaning it was not permanent. He starts right off with the question, "Did God cast off His people?" He answers with a resounding *God forbid!* Yet, Covenant Theology, because of its belief that God rejected Israel over *their* rejection of the Messiah, essentially responds with, "*Yes, God **did** fully and finally reject His people Israel.*"

To prove that the present rejection of Israel is temporary, Paul cites the fact that God has *always* had a Remnant for Himself (cf. Isaiah 10:22-23; Hosea 1:10). He has *never* been without a Remnant. At the same time, when a Jewish individual *receives* salvation and becomes part of the Church, he does *not* cease being Jewish. We must understand that Paul has so far been teaching that there are two Israels (but *both* are Jewish), and a Jewish person who comes to faith in Christ *continues* to be Jewish. To see anything else in this section of Romans is a total misunderstanding and misrepresentation of Paul's teaching here and elsewhere.

Paul speaks of the "mystery" to which he previously alluded, which is the "partial hardening" of Israel. This began at Christ's rejection and continues to this day. Some of the Israelites, like Paul, were *not* hardened in order that they might *receive* salvation. The rest of them *were* hardened.

Further, Paul teaches that despite the partial hardening during his day (and into today), *"the fullness is that in the future, there will be national salvation of Israel as a whole...there is a connection between the fullness of Israel and the fullness of the Gentiles. Note however that **the national salvation of Israel was not itself the mystery**"* [50] (emphasis added).

When Paul speaks regarding the future national salvation of Israel, he obviously *cannot* be referring to the Church, because the Church was already in existence. He is obviously then, referring to some future point in time when God will take the Remnant He will have set aside for Himself and place them within a restored Israel, *after* the Great Tribulation. Their salvation however, will come the same way that our salvation comes to us: through faith in Christ.

Ultimately, Paul is very glad to have a ministry with the Gentiles, because he believes that as more Gentiles come to faith in Christ, the more his fellow Jews will be provoked to jealousy, desiring that same faith. Paul uses the illustration of the Olive Tree (Romans 11:16-25) to drive this point home (*see **figure 9** next page*).

---

[50] Arnold G. Fruchtenbaum, *Footsteps of the Messiah* (San Antonio: Ariel Ministries 2003), 682

The Olive Tree - Romans 11:16-24

Romans 11:16

"And if the firstfruit is holy, so is the lump: and if the root is holy, so are the branches."

Meaning

The *firstfruit* and the *root* refer to Abraham, Isaac, and Jacob and the Abrahamic Covenant.

They are *holy* because they were separated and consecrated by God for a divine purpose.

Israel as a nation is the *lump* and the *branches*. The principle is based on Numbers 15:17-21: the holiness or consecration of the *firstfruit* and the *root* is passed on to the *lump* and the *branches*.

Just as the *firstfruit* sanctifies the whole harvest, the *lump*, even some day all Israel will also be sanctified.

The Olive Tree

The Olive Tree does not represent the Church or Israel.
- it represents a place of spiritual blessing

Israel is the owner of the Olive Tree (verses 23-24)

The root of this place of blessing is the Abrahamic Covenant. Paul makes this same point in Ephesians 2:11-16 and 3:5-6.

The Gentiles have been grafted into this place of blessing and are partakers of its sap. The Gentiles are not "takers-over", but partakers of Jewish spiritual blessings.

pages 784-786 in Footsteps

To sum up: in Romans 9-11, Paul is explaining two things about this mystery *not* known prior to his day:
1. Israel has been partially hardened
2. *Until* the fullness of the Gentiles has occurred

Until Then...

The word *until* is a preposition which is used to indicate a limited space of time. The use of the word *until* precludes permanence. It always alludes to something of a temporary nature.

In Wuest's Expanded Translation of the New Testament, the latter part of verse 25 of chapter 11 is virtually identical to what we read above in the *English Standard Version (ESV)*. Paul is *preempting* any idea that Israel's hardening is a *permanent condition* by using the word *until*. The idea of permanent rejection cannot be gained from the text without doing damage to it (and that includes allegorizing it to mean that Israel is essentially now the Church).

Paul is specifically speaking of a length of time called the "*fullness of the Gentiles,*" which clearly is to be seen as temporary, since it will come to an end (by the use of the word "until"). What does that mean except that Israel will *remain* partially hardened in their hearts *until* the last Gentile earmarked for salvation (this side of the Tribulation) comes in (to salvation). At some point in time after this, the Tribulation will begin and God will call out His Remnant through the same salvation that is available to us today. During this time, Gentiles will also be saved.

"All individual Jews who become believers during the seven years of the Tribulation are part of the Remnant of Israel. This includes the 144,000 Jews (Rev. 7) and those Jews of Jerusalem who become believers in the middle of the Tribulation (Rev. 11:13). It includes all individual Jews who become believers as a result of the preaching of the 144,000 or the Two Witnesses of Revelation 11. It also includes the Remnant of Revelation 12:17 that Satan will attack in a particular

way."⁵¹ These will then go in and possess the land, immediately after the Tribulation, and *during* the millennial reign of Christ.

During the present day, all Jews and all Gentiles need the salvation that is only found in Jesus Christ, made available through His death and resurrection. This salvation is based on faith in God alone. There is no other way to gain salvation, and there *never* has been. It is not by work of any kind, but by faith in Jesus' completed work as the perfect sacrificial Lamb. No one can earn salvation. Salvation could *never* be earned. We must *believe* God. Just as the Holy Spirit opened the eyes of the dying thief on the cross next to Jesus, enabling him to *believe* in Jesus, He also opens our eyes, enabling us to *believe*. It is all God. It is all *of* God. It is all *from* God. It is all *for* God's glory and it is due to His absolute sovereignty.

The gospel went out to the Gentiles directly *because* of Israel's unbelief (hardened heart) in order to *create* the Church, made up of both Jew and Gentile. It was *not* done because God had finally and completely rejected Israel. Paul states their hardening was and remains *partial* and *temporary*.

Why did God have to do it this way? Why could not God simply have chosen to offer the gospel to the Jewish people and the Gentiles as well; directly to both groups? Simply put, because God created the nation of Israel as His peculiar people (cf. Deuteronomy 7:7-8; 14:2; 2 Samuel 7:24; Psalm 33:12; Ezekiel 11:17; Isaiah 11:12; 43:1-28; Jeremiah 24:6; Amos 9:14; Zechariah 12:10). They *remain* His peculiar people, and when Jesus returns physically His very first order of business will be to rescue Israel from the tyranny of the Antichrist (cf. Revelation 19:11-21).

The nation of Israel was created for God's purposes, and certainly those purposes included being a light to the world (cf. Matthew 5:13-

---

⁵¹ Arnold G. Fruchtenbaum *Footsteps of the Messiah* (San Antonio: Ariel Ministries), 786

16). God had created Israel in order to bring people from all nations to Himself for salvation. The Gentiles would be able to approach God *through* the nation of Israel.

Israel's Purpose
Consider the fact that God had created Israel for a number of purposes, which are clearly seen in His Word. Israel was created to:

- Be a blessing to the world
- Recover lost humanity from Adam's and Eve's fall
- To fill the earth with God's glory

We see this in any number of places like, Psalm 72:17, Isaiah 11:9, and 40:5, and Habakkuk 2:14. Those who bless Israel are promised blessing. Those who curse Israel are promised to be cursed. God's *unconditional* election of Abram, and of the nation which came from him, remains in effect to this day (cf. Genesis 12:1-3; Galatians 3:8-16).

God created Israel as His peculiar treasure to be an example and a channel through which the rest of the world could be blessed. It was Israel's responsibility to be witnesses to the world. This was to have been by their obedience to God in His provided land. When they became disobedient, judgment usually followed, which normally resulted in the *loss* of that land temporarily. Therefore, Israel was supposed to show the world the measure of God's blessing through their obedience. Obviously, in order to fully obey, this willingness and obedience had to come from within, where their *belief* (or unbelief) was housed. The reason Israel disobeyed as often as she did was due to *unbelief*.

Israel was created so that the entire world of Gentiles would see and understand the blessings that stem from obedience to Him. The Gentiles would also become aware of the built-in curse of disobedience, which stemmed from *unbelief* (cf. Exodus 19:5-6; Deuteronomy 28;

29:24-29; I Kings 8:41-43; 9:4-9; 10:24; Isaiah 41:20; 42:6; 43:10-12, 21; 44:8; 60:3; Jeremiah 22:8-9; Zechariah 8:23; Mark 16:15; Acts 1:8; I Corinthians 10:11).

Because they failed, Israel was not much of a light at all. The only thing that routinely shined forth from them was their unbelief and resultant disobedience.

If we look at the many times Israel became disobedient, with her land being taken from her, we note clearly that God always returned her to that same land. Her sin was consistently against God. Her unfaithfulness resulted in being expelled from the land of Canaan, but God always brought her back to it.

Israel's Disobedience
Each of the episodes in which Israel lived in unbelief, which resulted in disobedience and finally removal from the land, always came full circle so that she found herself back in the land. This was normally the case after years of captivity, then crying out to God in repentance, then asking God for help.

Probably the most well known scenario is the time Israel became captive while living in Egypt. God brought them there through Joseph, who became the second in command over all of Egypt, under Pharaoh. From Joseph, and his brothers (who were the 12 patriarchs of what became the nation of Israel), a group of people numbering into the thousands eventually lived in Egypt (cf. Genesis 25-50).

At the beginning of the book of Exodus, we see that time has passed since Joseph, and there is a new Pharaoh. This particular Pharaoh apparently did not know of Joseph (cf. Exodus 1:8). He saw the burgeoning numbers of people of Israel and became fearful that they would be able to overthrow him one day. He made them slaves and put them to work creating brick for the many projects that he wanted created.

Eventually, the people began to chafe under this heavy workload and cried out to God for deliverance. He soon sent Moses who eventually led the Israelites out of their bondage and to the land of promise. Here they were to live for God, allowing Him to work through them to bring His salvation to the world of the Gentiles. We know that this is not what occurred. We know that Israel consistently failed God due to her consistent unbelief and rebellious ways.

With Israel as a nation, God would have to offer the gospel to the Gentiles *through* Israel. However, since Israel continually failed, she rarely stood as a model of God's love and salvation to the world.

When Israel rejected the Messiah, the result was another in a long line of judgments by God. Jesus Himself spoke of this coming judgment in Matthew 24, Mark 13, and Luke 21: the Olivet Discourse. This soon-to-be judgment took place in A.D. 70 when Roman armies destroyed Jerusalem and the Temple.

God became silent once again, where Israel was concerned. Their unbelief chased them out of the land and scattered them to places all over the world. This is no different from what Israel had experienced every time they rebelled against God. Judgment came in the form of an army, overcame the nation and either carried her into captivity or chased her into a dispersion.

Scraps to Dogs
When Jesus walked this earth during His public ministry, while He at times dealt with those outside the nation of Israel, His goal was to call the lost sheep of the house of Israel to Him (cf. Matthew 15:24). He offered Himself to them as King on the day He rode into Jerusalem on the back of a colt in what is normally termed the Triumphal Entry (cf. Matthew 21:1-11; Mark 11:1-11; Luke 19:29-44; John 12:12-19). Though the people placed palm branches in front of Him on the ground as He came into Jerusalem, nonetheless He was crucified only a few days later; His offer to be King of Israel was rejected.

Every time Israel disobeyed God, they were in fact, *rejecting Him.* To us, it may appear that they were not keeping the laws, or that they wanted a human king, but to God it is clear that Israel was rejecting Him. He said as much when the people clamored for a human king; someone who would sit on a physical throne. We read about this in the book of 1 Samuel 8. God's Words, which we read in verse seven are tragically sad, *"And the LORD said to Samuel, 'Obey the voice of the people in all that they say to you, for they have not rejected you, but they have rejected me from being king over them'."*

It is clear then that God was actually being rejected. This outward expression stemmed from the inner unbelief that they harbored.

This rejection of God is continually seen throughout the Old Testament. When we get to the New Testament, Israel's leaders did the same thing they had always done: rejected God in the form of Jesus. Israel had become complacent, proud, able to do things on her own, and did not feel that she needed anyone over her, unlike the time Israel had demanded that Samuel provide the nation with a king.

If each time Israel fell through unbelief resulting in disobedience, and the people wound up rejecting God, was there any real difference between all those other times of rejecting God and the time of rejecting God in Christ? It was ultimately *still* rejecting God and His rule over their lives.

Was It the Last Straw?
However, Covenant Theology maintains that rejecting Jesus was the last straw for God. This then, required Him to push Israel away from Him. Covenant Theology essentially believes that the start of the Church is found in the Old Testament, so when God transferred everything from Israel to the Church, it wasn't that He was rejecting Israel so much as He was merely emphasizing the Church and diminishing (to nothing) the role of Israel.

To this end, Berkhof comments, "The Old Testament employs two words to designate the Church, namely *qahal* (or *kahal*), derived from an obsolete root *qal* (or *kal*), meaning 'to call'; and *edhah*, from *ya'adh*, 'to appoint' or 'to meet or come together at an appointed place.' These two words are sometimes used indiscriminately, but were not, at first, strictly synonymous...Consequently we find on occasions the expression *qehal 'edhah*, that is, *'the assembly of the congregation' Ex. 12:6; Num. 14:5; Jer. 26:17."*[52]

As we can see, Berkhof seems to be arguing that the church existed in the Old Testament *within* Israel, so for God to put the emphasis on the Church is nothing that should be considered unusual. This is at the very least a stretch considering Paul's claims that the Church was a mystery revealed to him by Christ, as has been previously explained.

Israel's rejection of Christ appears to be of the same category as all of her past rejections of God, except for the fact that He was actually walking the earth. Once Israel rejected Jesus, God did what He normally did. He sent judgment and placed Israel on the shelf temporarily, to deal with them again at some future point in time.

It is because of this that Paul addresses Israel's partial hardening and blindness, which we are assured, is only temporary. God made them blind. He uses it so that He might bypass Israel completely and offer the gospel to the Gentiles *directly*. None of this means that God has finished working with Israel. It only means, according to Paul, that God deals **directly** with individual Gentiles, instead of having to reach them *through* the nation of Israel, since God has *temporarily* ceased to work with the nation of Israel.

There is *nothing* in the Old or New Testaments indicating that the gospel message was to remain with Israel only. Those who claim

---

[52] Louis Berkhof, *Systematic Theology* (Grand Rapids: Eerdmans 1996), 555

that Dispensationalism somehow teaches that God failed, base their understanding on an incorrect view of what Dispensationalism actually espouses.

In Christ, no one has to become part of the nation of Israel. We become part of the Body of Christ: the Church. In the Old Testament, salvation was found *through* the nation of Israel because that was how God chose to reveal Himself, not only to Israel but also to all the nations of the world.

Dr. Arnold Fruchtenbaum comments on this section of Scripture as well. He states, *"Paul shows that Israel's rejection of the Messiahship of Jesus did not mean that God's plan and program had come to naught, that it had fallen short, or that it had fallen aside; rather, this was all proceeding according to divine plan. It was in the program of God that Israel would reject the Messiahship of Jesus, and it is because of Israel's rejection of His Messiahship that mercy was extended to the Gentiles. The mercy shown to the Gentiles was not to the total exclusion of the Jews, however, because there is a Remnant coming to saving faith even among the Jews. There are vessels of mercy among both Jews and Gentiles, and there are vessels of wrath among both Jews and Gentiles. The reason the gospel went out freely among the Gentiles is because Israel as a nation had rejected it. It is something that God had already planned in the Old Testament, because what Paul teaches here is what Isaiah predicted in Isaiah 49:1-13."*[53]

The Will of God

We have seen that God's will includes many aspects. While salvation is absolutely part of it, so are many other things: *"And why do you worry about clothes? See how the lilies of the field grow. They do not labor or spin. Yet I tell you that not even Solomon in all his splendor was dressed like one of these. If that is how God clothes the grass of the*

---

[53] Arnold G. Fruchtenbaum *Footsteps of the Messiah* (San Antonio: Ariel Ministries), 777-778

field, which is here today and tomorrow is thrown into the fire, will he not much more clothe you, O you of little faith? So do not worry, saying, 'What shall we eat?' or 'What shall we drink?' or 'What shall we wear?' For the pagans run after all these things, and your heavenly Father knows that you need them. But seek first his kingdom and his righteousness, and all these things will be given to you as well. Therefore do not worry about tomorrow, for tomorrow will worry about itself. Each day has enough trouble of its own" (Matthew 5:28-34).

Christ is explaining that when we worry, we are not glorifying God. When we worry, we are showing little to no faith in God's ability to provide for us. Worry also questions God's sovereignty. It says "*I doubt that God can provide. He's not big enough. This problem is too large for Him to handle.*"

If we turn to Scofield's own notes regarding God's sovereignty, we read "*Election is therefore: (1) the sovereign act of God in grace whereby certain are chosen from among mankind for Himself (John 15. 19), (2) the sovereign act of God whereby certain elect persons are chosen for distinctive service for Him (Lk. 6. 13; Acts 9. 15; 1 Cor. 1. 27, 28).*"[54] Scofield defines predestination as "*that effective exercise of the will of God by which things before determined by Him are brought to pass.*"[55]

In many of Scofield's notes throughout the Bible, he attests to the full sovereignty of God. For instance, in a note for Psalm 2, Scofield admonishes regarding the "*derision of Jehovah (v.4) that men should suppose it possible to set aside His covenant (2 Sam. 7. 8-17), and oath (Psa. 89. 34-37).*"[56]

---

[54] Rev. C. I. Scofield, D.D. *Scofield Study Bible* (New York: Oxford University Press, 1909, 1917), 1311
[55] Ibid, 1250
[56] Rev. C. I. Scofield, D.D. *Scofield Study Bible* (New York: Oxford University Press, 1909, 1917), 600

He also states, regarding this very same Psalm, *"Trust is the characteristic O.T. word for the N.T. 'faith,' 'believe.' It occurs 152 times in the O.T., and is the rendering of Heb. words signifying to take refuge (e.g. Ruth 2.12); to lean on (e.g. Psa. 56.3); to roll on (e.g. Psa. 22.8); to stay upon (e.g. Job 35.14).*[57]

In Romans 9:17, Paul highlights God's sovereignty by quoting Exodus 9:16: *"For the Scripture says to Pharaoh, 'For this very purpose I have raised you up, that I might show my power in you, and that my name might be proclaimed in all the earth'."*

God's Highest Purpose
Did you read that carefully? God brought Pharaoh into this world for one purpose. God used Pharaoh to show His *power*, in order that His Name would be known throughout the world! Here is a case of a person being brought into this world for ultimately one purpose, and it is the highest possible purpose that exists for any part of God's Creation: *to showcase God's sovereignty*. In other words, Pharaoh wound up glorifying God even though he certainly did not *want* to do it, nor did he do it *voluntarily*. He glorified God when God displayed His power and sovereignty *over* Pharaoh. There is *nothing* in there indicating anything about salvation.

Throughout the entire Old Testament, we are *encouraged* to give Him the glory. In Exodus 14, we see God's determinate will to gain glory *through* Pharaoh, an event that Paul reminds us of in Romans 9:17. In other places like 1 Chronicles 16, we are told that we should ascribe to God the glory due His Name. Why is glory due His Name? Because He is sovereign.

Psalm 19 tells us that God's glory is shown in the handiwork of the heavens and in His Creation. Throughout many other Psalms, we are told to sing songs of praise, which bring glory to Him. No one else

---

[57] Ibid

should receive any glory that is due only to God. Why? Because God is fully sovereign. He is absolutely in control. No one else can even come close to His sovereignty in their own character, especially considering the fact that everything that exists does so because God created it (cf. 1 John 1:3; also Colossians 1:15-20).

This fact makes the desires of Satan and others even more pitiful. The idea that a *created* being of any type would somehow be able to rise *above* its Creator defies all logic. Yet, such is the consequence of ego. Satan fell because of it, as did Adam and Eve. Pharaoh and many others tried to stand against God, but were shown (in God's own good time) the futility of their puny efforts.

Under God's Mighty Hand of Judgment
The result of the Israelites' unbelief was *rebellion*. Though they had escaped the slavery and depravity of Egypt only because God's love and grace made that possible, they failed to enter into the land of Canaan because of their unbelief, leading to rebellion.

The result of their rebellion was temporary banning from the land before they could even take hold of it. God forced them to wander in the wilderness for forty years. This allowed all the men who saw God's glory and signs, which had been performed since their days in Egypt, would *not* see the Promised Land. They would die in the wilderness (cf. Numbers 14:20ff), because of their rebellion.

Please also note that in verse twenty-one of Numbers 14, immediately after the Lord pardons them because of Moses' prayer, He states quite succinctly. *"Indeed, as I live, all the earth will be filled with the glory of the Lord"* (NASB). Everything, at some point in time, will glorify the Lord by *proclaiming* His absolute sovereignty. This is clear in the Old as well as the New Testaments (cf. Isaiah 45:23-24; Philippians 2:9-11).

By far, the most egregious problem in Mr. Gillespie's beliefs is that it is *he* who unfortunately ends up is *demeaning* God's sovereignty. He falls into this trap because he is clearly confusing God's *plan* for Israel with God's *salvation* for them.

Salvation for the Jew and Gentile
There is no doubt that God created the Church and that within the Church are believers of all nations, including individuals of *Jewish* origin. This is obvious in the book of Acts, beginning with chapter two. Here, after the Holy Spirit descends upon those in the Upper Room, they went out and were immediately accused of being drunk by some who saw them.

Peter responded to the crowd in the very first sermon *after* the creation of the Church. Three thousand people became believers that day, after hearing Peter's sermon! Three thousand people! Most of these were undoubtedly Jewish because they were visiting for the celebration of Pentecost. They would have come to Jerusalem from many parts of the then known world for this celebration and would return home afterwards.

God worked mightily that day, using Peter's sermon literally to "prick the hearts of the hearers" (cf. Acts 2:37 KJV). This pricking of their consciences (hearts) was enough to cause many of them to reach out to God in faith. Their eyes were opened to the truth of what Peter was telling them, and because of that they received Christ as Savior *and* Messiah and their new life in Him began.

Since that time, we are aware that Peter opened the door (through the direction of the Spirit) to preach the gospel to the Gentiles (cf. Acts 10). However, it was Paul whose ministry was directed toward Gentiles in large measure. Now, does this mean that the Jews no longer needed to hear the gospel? Of course not. It simply meant that God's *plan* for Paul was that he takes the message of the gospel to the Jews first, then the Gentiles.

Paul had tried repeatedly to take the message to Jews, but was always rejected, though some Jews did hear and believe. Reading the book of Acts carefully, we note that wherever Paul went, he always presented the gospel to Jews in the synagogue *first*, but he always wound up preaching to the Gentiles, too. He soon had a greater ministry to the Gentiles than to his own fellow Jews.

It is likely that all of these experiences and his feelings about them and his brethren played a large part in how the Lord used him to write the book of Romans. We will get to that later on in this book also, so hang on.

It is apparent that God was creating a new body of people, which would be composed of people from all walks of life, all cultures, and both genders. This would be the Church, the Bride of Christ.

The prophets *knew* that the gospel would go out to the Gentiles. What they did *not* know was that a new *body of believers was to be created* and that new body would be called *the Church*. They were *not* aware of this. As far as the prophets were concerned, they believed that the gospel would go out to the Gentile *from within* the nation of Israel, because that was how it was *supposed to be*.

Salvation to All

If salvation is offered to all as only *one* method, that would mean that when God saves anyone – Jew, Gentile, man, or woman – He does it by crediting righteousness to them based on their *faith* in Him. If that is the way He grants salvation, then it does not necessarily follow that the Church and Israel *are* mutually exclusive, as Covenant Theology believes.

Jewish individuals today who receive Christ become Jewish Christians: believers in Christ's substitutionary death and resultant resurrection. When Gentile individuals today receive Christ, they become Gentile Christians.

Both Jews and Gentiles who *fail* to receive Christ in this life before entering the next have the *same* exact place to look forward to: *hell*. This is not a reassuring picture for anyone.

Witnessing to the Jewish Person
Years ago, when I was putting myself through college, I found employment at a men's clothing store. It was a nice, family-owned operation where more upscale clothing was sold: shirts, pants, suits, etc. The owners were Jewish and they prided themselves on offering the latest styles and providing good customer service.

Every month or so, the window mannequins would require new outfits and the window dressing themselves would need to be updated. When the time for that came, another Jewish man and his son would come to the store from New York City and work on the windows.

During the slow times, we would chat. It was usually interesting conversation. I remember, after learning that he was Jewish, turning the conversation to the subject of Judaism and Christianity. I quickly learned that he was Jewish by ancestry, but not because he necessarily believed in Judaism, the Law, or that there was (and had been) a Messiah for the nation of Israel.

His understanding of Judaism was minimal. As we talked, I brought up the subject of Moses and the Law, just to hear what he would say. For him, it was not only distant, but it was obvious that he had a very difficult time believing any of it, which to me was tragic.

The windows were going to take a number of days to change out, which required him to return to the store every day for roughly a week. This gave me a great opportunity to discuss Judaism with him. Do not get me wrong; it was not my intention to lead him to a point of recognizing that he should get back into Judaism. I was hoping to find some common ground, something that I could use to point him to Christ and His substitutionary atonement. I felt that by introducing aspects of the Law and the sacrificial system, I would eventually find a good segue into a discussion of Jesus as Savior.

What I found instead was someone who was essentially an agnostic but who was moving toward the atheistic side of things. It was becoming a bit frustrating for me, but I kept on with it. I made sure that I waited on customers and I made certain that my conversation did not become too loud. Consequently, the conversations we had were for brief moments of time and that added to my frustration.

Over the course of the week, I was able to share with him my faith and what it meant to me: the fact that Jesus had died for my sin, offering salvation that I otherwise would not be able to enjoy. He seemed unimpressed. At one point, he stated that he did not believe in God and he was not worried about it.

Looking at him then, I simply said, "When you die, let's say that the God of the Bible *does* exist and you find yourself standing before Him in judgment. What will you do then?"

You have to understand that this man had an interesting personality, which tends to develop in people who live in large cities. He was joking around, kidding with the other workers, and you could tell that he liked to live life. Therefore, when he responded, I was not too surprised at what I heard. He said simply, with a slight twinkle in his, "*I would say 'I'm sorry,' and ask Him for forgiveness.*"

I just looked at him and said, "*Yeah, but by then it will be absolutely too late. Today He offers His forgiveness and salvation. Today is the day to receive the Lord.*" He laughed nervously, and excused himself to get back to work.

There is no other way. It is *not* one way for the Jew (or the OT saint) and another way for the Gentile, any more than it is one way for a man and another way for a woman. A man and a woman need the exact same thing to become Christians. They need *faith* in Christ's finished work on Calvary's cross. As I have said already a number of times, God's plan *involves* salvation, but that is not *all* that it involves.

Lucifer, Adam, Eve, and the Rest
When Lucifer sinned, God did not immediately destroy him, nor did He cast him into the bottomless pit. He certainly could have, but chose not to do so. When Adam and Eve sinned, while God tossed them out of the Garden of Eden, he did not simply lock them in outer darkness and throw away the key.

How about Cain? He is noted for being the first murderer (cf. John 8:44). Did God destroy him right then and there? No, but He certainly could have done so.

When David sinned by committing adultery and murdering Bathsheba's husband, Uriah the Hittite, what did God do (cf. 2 Samuel 11)? God indicated that judgment would fall and it would include the son of David and Bathsheba. God also indicated that the sword would not depart from David's house. Did God immediately kill David? Did God immediately, or at the end of his life, eventually send David to hell?

Samson was the last of the judges found in the book of Judges. He was all brawn, but he seemed to be lacking in the cranial department. He toyed with his power, as if it was something that should not be protected or cherished. He fell, and he fell hard, which resulted in having his eyes gouged out and becoming a weakling. However, at the end of his life, God answered his prayer and for one final act of retribution: God gave him the power literally to bring down the temple of the Philistines.

Moses (beginning Exodus 1ff), is an individual who probably had the closest relationship to God out of any other man on this earth (save Christ). After many years of walking with God, he messed up by striking the rock that God had commanded him simply to speak to. This is something God forgave, but the consequences *remained*.

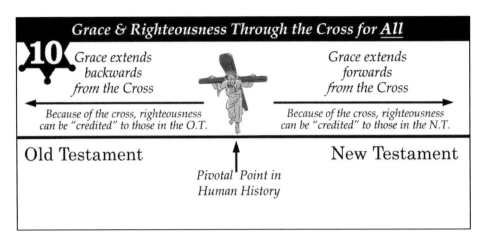

We can read about these individuals and more in what is termed the "Hall of Faith" in Hebrews 11. Here we see people who lived life, sought God, were dedicated to His service, but many of whom fell (and some fell badly, headlong) into grievous sin. God *never* rejected any of them and in fact, in spite of their sin, many of them are listed as people who were righteous and who exhibited faith in God.

Yet, Covenant Theology tells us that Israel *failed* and was rejected *permanently*. Does this not state that because Israel failed, then *God* failed, which is the very same thing Dispensationalism is charged with espousing? If Israel failed, then God failed, because they were His *chosen* people.

Paul continues to talk about Israel in Romans and the promises that will *yet* be fulfilled in them as a nation - not as individuals, and *not* in the Church. Paul believed then that God had specific plans for Israel as a nation that would not be fulfilled in the Church. These are two completely different entities.

Speaking for myself, when I attended PCB, I was taught that God is, above all, fully sovereign! In fact, Scofield himself echoes this thought when he states *"But we must not conclude that the wickedness of man has baffled the deliberate purpose of God, for His counsels include a second advent of His Son, when the predictions concerning*

Messiah's earthly glory will receive the same precise and literal fulfillment as did those which concerned His earthly sufferings."[58]

Love Produces Right Action

It is no different from husbands and wives who truly love one another. These individuals will willingly *do* things for each other based on that love. They do not "love" one another out of duty, which is no love at all. Their love is *seen* in their action. It is an automatic response to the love felt. It is a pleasure to do things for them.

It is clear from the Old Testament alone that men of faith (as Scofield calls them) loved Jehovah with all their heart and mind. Nothing else would prompt them to give up all and serve Him.

God has *never* failed; not once. He could not be God and fail. He did not fail when He created Lucifer, who eventually became the Christian's worst nightmare, Satan. God did not fail when He created Adam and Eve, knowing that they *would* fail and bring sin into the world.

God did not fail when He created the nation of Israel, in spite of the fact that *they* failed constantly, ultimately rejecting God the Son as their Messiah.

As shown by the chart (**Figure 10**), the cross of Christ is the central focus of all of human history. It is the point at which a full pardon and cancelation of debt was made possible and offered to men. Receiving that pardon meant receiving salvation.

God's grace through the cross of Christ allows God to "look back," crediting Abraham and others with righteousness, based on their faith in Him. He works this exact same way (with God looking forward) with believers today and into the future.

---

[58] http://www.biblebelievers.com/scofield/scofield_rightly03.html

Chapter 7
Grace Without Human Effort

I have tried to show that words can be easily taken out of their original context and redefined by people who unfortunately predicate their understanding of Dispensationalism on the misrepresentations often highlighted within Covenant Theology.

Over time, these same folks have come up with what they feel are effective rebuttals to Dispensationalism. Unfortunately, upon closer inspection it becomes clear that they are merely drawing conclusions based on *errant* or *misunderstood* information. They then misrepresent Dispensationalism, making *it* appear to be a lie.

Regarding this particular issue, we find Mr. Gillespie at odds with Dr. Lewis Sperry Chafer. Note first the statement by Dr. Chafer, followed by Gillespie's comments: *"As before stated, whatever God does for sinful men on any terms whatsoever [being made possible through the death of Christ] is to that extent, an act of divine grace; for whatever God does on the ground of Christ's death is gracious in character, and all will agree that a divine covenant which is void of all human elements is more gracious in character than one which is otherwise. These distinctions apply only to the divine side of the covenant. On the human side... there is no exercise of grace in any case; but the human requirements which the divine covenant imposes may be either absolutely lacking, or some so drastically imposed as to determine the destiny of the individual."*[59]

Responding to the above quote, Gillespie says, "*Chafer, in keeping with the standard definition of a dispensation,* **sees the Atonement as making grace possible throughout the various ages, which allows salvation to be viewed as gracious regardless of the added requirements of that specific dispensation.** *So, under Grace (...the human requirements which the divine covenant imposes may be either absolutely lacking...) if one can generate the necessary faith one might receive grace. Under the dispensation of Law (...or some so drastically imposed as to determine the destiny of the individual.), one might be required to keep the Law,*"[60] (emphasis added).

Reading Gillespie is frustrating because he is *so* close to actually understanding what Dispensationalism espouses, yet he still misses it. If Gillespie did *not* view God's plan as *only* salvific in nature, he probably would have understood what Chafer was. Chafer never said anything about conjuring up faith at all in order to possibly receive grace, yet Gillespie seems to think that he did. This confusion is continually represented by Gillespie's *misstatements* regarding both Dispensationalism and those who support it.

---

[59] http://www.inchristalone.org/ProblemsDispen.htm
[60] Ibid

Gillespie continues by stating, "*This issue is subtle but very significant. Notice the language in this quote: 'making grace possible.' To me this is one of the more insidious problems with dispensationalism. While it speaks of salvation by grace, it actually redefines grace. Grace in the biblical and orthodox sense is unmerited favor. But in the Dispensational sense it is favor that is merited. God offers the 'gift' of salvation differently in various dispensations. One's reception of this 'gift' is determined by whether the 'requirements of that specific dispensation' are met. This means that one pays for the gift through obedience. The pernicious dimension of this is that dispensationalism uses all the orthodox language of salvation by grace through faith, but in many cases, does not mean the same thing. It is really grace obtained through obedience. Too many groups today have inherited or adopted this definition of grace.*"[61]

Again though, what Chafer actually said was "*being made possible through the death of Christ.*" This is 100% true. In essence, Chafer is saying that *without* grace, salvation is *impossible*. This is also true.

Unfortunately, the continuing difficulty is that Gillespie *believes* that Chafer and others are *redefining grace*. In actuality, what Chafer is saying is that God is able to work on man's behalf at all *because of grace*. Chafer is **not** saying that *grace is possible if the necessary faith can be conjured up*.

Gillespie continues making the same error that he has made previously. He is confusing *salvation* with responsibilities or requirements that God places on individuals within specific dispensations. These are *not* the same thing at all. No one *earns* salvation in *any* dispensation, ever.

It is unfortunate that Chafer is made out to be an agent of subterfuge. Notice the comment: "*To me this is one of the more insidious problems with dispensationalism. While it speaks of salvation by grace, it actually redefines grace.*"

---

[61] http://www.inchristalone.org/ProblemsDispen.htm

Grace *is unmerited favor* and frankly, I do not see where Chafer is saying something different. What Chafer appears to be saying is that the *only reason* God is *able* to be gracious toward men at all is *because* of the death of Christ. So far, so good. Chafer then continues by stating, *"all will agree that a divine covenant which is void of all human elements is more gracious in character than one which is otherwise."* God did all the work, requiring nothing of man.

However, why does Gillespie seem to have a problem with the phrase *"making grace possible"*? It is solely because he *assumes* (and even *argues*) that Chafer is saying God only makes grace possible insofar as *man does* or *does not* have the necessary faith. This is, in fact, *not* what Chafer said.

Peter said this, *"For Christ also suffered once for sins, the righteous for the unrighteous,* **that he might bring us to God***, being put to death in the flesh but made alive in the spirit"* (1 Peter 3:18; emphasis added).

Is Peter saying that God is somehow dependent upon humanity? Peter definitely said, "that He (Christ) **might** bring us to God." If we follow the same logic as Gillespie, then we would have to accuse Peter of being deliberately insidious.

Here is a definition of salvation from Wikipedia, *"According to Christian belief,* **salvation is made possible by the life, death, and resurrection of Christ***, which in the context of salvation is referred to as the 'atonement'."*[62] I emphasized part of that quote to show that when people think of Christian salvation, they normally express it in terms similar to those. I have no idea who the person is who wrote the Wikipedia definition, much less, whether he or she is even Christian. The article included a look at salvation as seen through the eyes of many religions.

---

[62] http://en.wikipedia.org/wiki/Salvation

It is not out of the ordinary to hear statements like the following from Christians: "Jesus made my salvation possible." No one who heard that would stop the person and ask, "*What do you mean? Are you in fact saying that you were able to conjure up the required faith?!*" People automatically understand that when a person says, "Jesus made my salvation possible," what they are saying is that "*if it had not been for the sacrificial work of Jesus Christ on Calvary's cross, I would not have salvation. It is only by His grace that salvation for me is a possibility.*"

No one misunderstands a person to be saying that it was *their* own *faith* that somehow saved them! This is certainly not something Dispensationalists say regarding salvation.

Let us look at Gillespie's full quote regarding Chafer. He states, "*Chafer, in keeping with the standard definition of a dispensation,* **sees the Atonement as making grace possible throughout the various ages, which allows salvation to be viewed as gracious regardless of the added requirements of that specific dispensation**." Even though Gillespie *wrote* that quote, commenting on Chafer, he appears not to understand what he wrote. He is saying *exactly* what Dispensationalists believe about each of the various Dispensations. I could not have said it better myself. This is how humanity received salvation in *all* of the Dispensations, by God's grace. Any added requirements from one Dispensation to the next did not alter the means of receiving salvation one iota. They added requirements had no impact on salvation, but were merely additional responsibilities for *life*.

What Chafer states, is *exactly* what the atonement *does* provide! It was Christ's death, which made salvation possible at all in *all* ages. The real problem though, is that Gillespie, who seems to have the difficulty to start with, seems to be looking so earnestly for errors from Dispensationalists, that even when he says exactly what salvation is (as stated by a Dispensationalist), he finds reason to find error in it. This is truly disheartening.

Gillespie says, "*So, under Grace…if one can generate the necessary faith one might receive grace.*" Where did Chafer state or imply that? He seems to think it is in the statement "*the human requirements which the divine covenant imposes may be either absolutely lacking…*" The difficulty here is that the quote from Chafer does not seem to be a complete quote to begin with, which would then make it a quote out of context. Unfortunately, the references for this particular quote in the original document on the Internet were incorrect.

Clearly, even in partially quoting Chafer, the truth of what is stated is that the death of Christ has made *any* grace for salvation available at all! He further states that this graciousness, which stemmed from the cross, is *without* human requirements ("void of all human elements"). In the end then, it seems clear enough that Lewis Sperry Chafer is stating that salvation is a free gift of God, made possible *only* by the grace of God in Christ, and there is absolutely nothing that man can do to earn it.

It is difficult not to wonder why Gillespie, who is obviously from the Covenant Theology side of the tracks, did not go to *other* works by Chafer to ferret out what it is that Chafer is actually saying. Chafer has written much on the subject.

For instance, in the 7th volume of his *Systematic Theology*, Chafer spends some time summarizing each of the doctrines. In his summary of salvation, he states the following: "*2. The Work of God. Two Old Testament passages indicate the "salvation belongeth unto the Lord" (Ps. 3:8), "salvation is of the Lord" (Jonah 2:9).* **Any system which tends to combine human responsibility with this divine undertaking is wrong**. *Ephesians 2:8-10 relates good works to salvation* *wrought by grace as an effect thereof, and not a cause"*[63] (emphasis added).

This *should be* clear enough to show Chafer is teaching that salvation is *wholly* and *completely* a work of God. To eradicate any doubt, here is another quote from the same work and which should clarify things even further: *"4. One Condition. About 115 passages condition salvation on believing alone, and about 35 simply on faith. There are certain things, however, often added by man to this one and only condition, like the following: believe and repent, believe and be baptized, believe and confess sin, believe and confess Christ publicly, believe and promise a better manner of life, believe and pray for salvation."*[64]

Still, there are those who believe that *the following* is what Dispensationalism actually teaches: *"There are three components which identify every dispensation: 1) It begins with a new divine revelation; 2) A certain span of time which it covers; 3)* **Specific requirements of salvation for those in that time period***. Various sects and cults took this scheme and applied it to the Church Age. They said that within Church history God makes salvation available through progressive revelation and human response to the given revelation. Notice how this scheme describes the initial pattern followed by every Christian sect. Since God deals with humanity differently in every dispensation there must be a new revelation discovered and proclaimed so that people know how to be saved in that dispensation. The system sets up unwary Christians to look past the already revealed Gospel (as understood through justification), to something ever newly revealed,"*[65] (emphasis added).

This quote is wrong in a number of areas. Dispensationalism does *not* teach various forms of salvation at all (and I apologize for repeating myself so often). The requirements God gave to man during each

---

[63] Lewis Sperry Chafer, *Systematic Theology, Vol 7* (Grand Rapids: Kregel Publications 1976), 273
[64] Ibid, 274
[65] http://www.inchristalone.org/ProblemsDispen.htm

specific age have *nothing* to do with salvation. They have everything to do with the blessings that come from obeying God from the heart. This also provides a greater *awareness* of how salvation *works* and what it *provides*.

If one would stop to consider that the requirements *given* by God within each of the various dispensations are nothing more than *job requirements,* it might be easier to grasp. These job requirements have *nothing* to do with *salvation*, and everything to do with *remaining in fellowship with God*.

Consider it this way: when we go to work, what is our number one objective? It is normally to please the boss, isn't it? We want to please the boss by doing things his way. This ensures our continued success in the company. Employees who do terrible work (or no work at all), usually are not employed for long.

Each job description comes with specific *responsibilities* that the employer expects to be followed. Failure to follow them can result in anything from a verbal warning, to a written warning, to firing, which for our purposes relates to being out of fellowship with God (not loss of salvation).

Look at **figures 11** and **12**. The first chart titled, "Your Jobs throughout Your Life" represents the numerous jobs a person holds throughout his life. As can be seen, each job has different and often greater responsibilities associated with it. For instance, mowing people's lawns includes responsibilities like keeping the lawn mower in good running condition, taking care to mow people's lawns well, and edging the lawns just as well. This certainly does not compare to the level of responsibility that one has when attending college. There is much more on the line here, with studying a great deal, balancing time between classes so that all assignments are covered, making

✪ Your Jobs Throughout Your Life

(Various "Dispensations" Require Different Job Responsibilities)

POINT IN LIFE	CAREER PATH	RESPONSIBILITIES
Age 26	Offered partnership in the engineering firm	Responsible for specific customers, job deadlines, oversee specific number of employee and jobs
Age 24	Engineering internship	Work hard, continue studying, never be late, don't complain
Age 22	Shoe salesman	Respect customers, work hard, keepo track of inventory
Age 18 - 22	College to be an electrical engineer	Study hard, work odd jobs for money, pay for college
Age 16	Paper Route	Papers to customers, collect money, keep bike in good working condition
Age 10	Mow Lawns	Keep lawn mower in good shape; do job well
Birth - Age 0	Eat, sleep, grow	

The Blessings of Your Job and Its Requirements

A — Great productivity leads to accolades, career expansion and pay increases.

B — Poor productivity leads to verbal, or written warnings, poor reviews and potential firing

Arrive to Work!

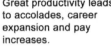
Ready to Go

Not Ready to Go

Completed Project Research on Time

Incomplete Research for Project at Deadline

Great Presentation to Client!

Forgot About Client Meeting!

Great job!

You're Fired!

sure bills are paid to the college on time, getting enough sleep and much more. Anyone who has been to college knows how it works. However, once college is over, with that electrical engineering degree under your belt, it's time for a job in that field. If one cannot be obtained, another job might be an option until a job in the electrical engineering field becomes available. Once there, the responsibilities of that job can often be *huge*. There are CAD programs to use in the design of the electrical circuitry for the project that is being worked on. There are employees to relate to, as well as clients. Things must be done in a timely manner, or you risk losing the client the next time they need something. As we grow, normally so does the responsibility that comes into our life.

The next chart, "The Blessings of Your Job and Its Responsibilities," breaks this down even further. Note that in any work situation, each employee has a role to play and that same employee has two options regarding how he will handle his workload. Plan A shows the employee who is on time to work, ready to go, does the research necessary for each project, and finishes it on time. This allows him to present his findings to the client, which in turn allows the client to make the best choice possible. An employee like this normally deserves and receives accolades, which can eventually turn into career advancement and pay raises.

Notice Plan B though. This employee is never ready to go, always has excuses, never completes the research for projects on time, and even completely forgets about the upcoming meeting with the client! Obviously, the client will think twice before opting to come to the company where the employee under Plan B works. His poor job performance results in verbal or written warnings. If it continues, this employee may find himself out of a job.

The various dispensations simply show us that God gave humanity *more* responsibilities within each. He rightfully expected man to live up to those responsibilities. Those within Israel who did were often blessed. This often resulted in the ability to overcome enemies on the battlefield, continued health, greater knowledge, more blessed worship, etc.

Those who failed time after time to follow the requirements given by God were warned, warned again, and often warned yet again. Finally, after God decided that He had provided enough opportunity, He withdrew His blessing. This often resulted in Israel being overrun by foreign entities, in which Israelites were killed or captured. Usually this also included taking over the land of Israel, or removing the Israelites from it, or both.

Please note though that in either case, those who rebelled frequently were simply *not* saved to begin with, and it showed in their demeanor toward God. Those who *were* saved also proved it by their attitude and actions toward God and one another.

The responsibilities found within each dispensation had nothing to do with *how* a person received salvation! It is really, so simple to understand **IF** it is first understood that faith is the basis for any relationship with God at all. Those who had faith in God also had salvation. This showed in their approach to God. Look, as merely one example, of the 12 spies that Moses sent out. Of them, only two of them – Joshua and Caleb – believed in God's faithfulness and sovereignty. Only those two had the faith that pleased God and they had that faith because God opened their eyes to the truth. This *resulted* in faith in God. Notice the 10 who did *not* have the necessary faith in God. Their fear took hold of them and they were unable to believe that God could save them. Was their unbelief based on reality? Of course not, yet it stymied their ability to please God. What was the result? The people moaned and groaned and God decided that they would wander in the wilderness for 40 years until all the grumblers were dead.

After they had all died in the wilderness, Israel then headed back toward Canaan, but this time they went in. Who led them? Joshua. It was the same Joshua who 40 years before had believed that God was able to and would give them the victory! He was rewarded for the faith that he already possessed in God. He possessed it because he had salvation.

Along with salvation, we as Christians are justified in God's sight. In speaking of justification, Chafer said, *"Justification is a declaration by God respecting the Christian that he has been made forever right and acceptable to Himself. For so much as this to be declared there must be an unalterable reality on which it may rest. This basis is the position to which the Christian has been brought through God's grace. All whom God has predetermined are called, and all who are called are justified, and all who are justified are now (logically speaking), and to be (chronologically speaking), glorified (Rom. 8:29-30)."*[66]

Unfortunately, the problem that the Covenant Theologian *says* exists within dispensationalist writings in actuality, do not exist at all. However, it does not appear that this confusion within the Covenant Theology camp will go away until they stop seeing subterfuge in the writings of authors like Ryrie, Chafer, and others. If people can misquote and misrepresent Chafer, Scofield, Ryrie, and others, it then becomes understandable how they can so misrepresent God's Word, which is a far greater error.

---

[66] Lewis Sperry Chafer, *Systematic Theology, Vol. 7* (Grand Rapids: Kregel Publications 1976), 219-220

Chapter 8
Espousing Fear?

This chapter deals with another one of the problems that Covenant Theology has with aspects of Dispensationalism. Here is Mr. Gillespie again: *"Lastly, I am very concerned that the teaching of dispensationalism is **not essentially comforting**. It is not good news that God's plan has been thwarted in the past. It is not good news that God had to come up with an alternative plan since Israel rejected Christ. It makes the Gospel sound like plan B. There is another aspect of this that might be quite sensitive to readers of this paper. It's the way that too many dispensationalists teach the Second Coming of*

Christ. Their presentation is oriented toward fear for the Christian rather than faith."[67] (emphasis added)

I think it would be best if I took this quote apart and dealt with it step by step. I will begin with the first sentence.

1. *"Lastly, I am very concerned that the teaching of dispensationalism is not essentially comforting."*

However, this is no reason to discount the plausibility of a biblical doctrine. It is a fact that *Jesus Christ spoke more of hell* than He did about any other subject. Hell is not a comforting doctrine. Just *because* something is not comforting, it does not necessarily mean that it is *not* correct.

We could take Noah as an example. For 120 years, he preached one thing: that God was going to destroy the earth with a global flood. The only survivors would be found inside the Ark that he and his sons were building. In all seriousness, would Mr. Gillespie accuse Jesus or Noah of not having a comforting message? One would certainly hope not.

Yet, another question that must be asked is, what exactly is so uncomfortable about eternity that Christians need to fear? The idea that Dispensationalism supposedly teaches a fear-inducing message is one that is *not* directed at those who truly know Jesus Christ as Savior. The message of coming judgment is directed at those who, as in Noah's day, were given all the signs, heard all the warnings, and yet in spite of all that, disregarded the truth of Noah's message. Truth is truth, and if it induces fear in people, so be it.

Lastly, on this note, one wonders if Mr. Gillespie believes in the doctrine of eternal punishment. Certainly, the doctrine of eternal punishment is not at all comforting, yet it is something that is reserved

---

[67] http://www.inchristalone.org/ProblemsDispen.htm

for those who die without having received Jesus as Savior. Entering into the next life without the protection that salvation offers is not comforting in the least, yet that is the only alternative to salvation.

Is Mr. Gillespie saying that the doctrine of eternal punishment should *not* be preached from the pulpit, nor should it be written about in books? Is this because it is not at all comforting?

It is likely that Noah did *not* preach this: *"Folks, I need you to be aware that you are all going to die. God will open up the gates of the clouds and the earth and water will flood this entire planet. It will completely engulf you and you will all die in the coming flood. Thank you for being here. I bid you good evening."*

I cannot imagine Noah preaching that and then simply walking away, only to come back the next day and preach the *same* type of message. Obviously, Noah presented both sides of the same coin. Judgment was coming, but God was using Noah to create a way out for anyone who wanted to receive it.

Jesus did the same thing. He presented both sides of the same coin, speaking about hell at one point, but also presenting the way of escape.

For Lot, it was a bit different, but the same basic thing applied to him as well (though he was the *recipient* of the message, not its presenter). The angels who were sent by God to destroy Sodom and Gomorrah made sure to get Lot to safety first. All of this can be found in Genesis 19, with background leading up to it beginning in Genesis 13. The angels came and essentially preached the message of God's impending judgment. They also informed Lot that they came to take him and his family safely away. There was obviously a serious time-constraint here because the text indicates that the angels told Lot at least twice essentially to "hurry up!" The text states, *"Escape [to*

Zoar] quickly, for I can do nothing till you arrive there" (Genesis 19:22).

The Dispensationalist does the same thing when discussing the End Times. The outline of God's coming judgment is presented, along with the way of escape, which is salvation through Christ. Of course, there is great debate over the Rapture: whether it is a real doctrine, or one made up; if it is real, does it take place before, during or after the Tribulation? What about the Second Coming; doesn't Jesus return only *once*? If so, why the Rapture? There are all types of questions and the answers are fairly easy to explain.

The truth is that the Rapture is really patterned after Enoch in a number of ways. *"Enoch walked with God, and he was not, for God took him"* (Genesis 5:24). Have you ever wondered *why* God simply *took* Enoch? The sense is that Enoch did not see death, but was literally "translated," and this was *prior* to the judgment of a global flood on the earth.

If that does not work for you, then we have Noah himself. Noah preached 120 years and then what happened? God said it was time and shut him up safely in the Ark (cf. Genesis 7:16). What is interesting here are two things.

1. *God closed up the Ark*
2. *God did not release His judgment upon the earth until all were safely inside the Ark*

If it is true – what the Bible states about the End Times and the coming judgment – then the comfort is found in the *Rapture*. However, even if the Rapture does not take place, comfort is *still* found in Christ.

Think of the many thousands of Christians who have died in Christ's Name. The landscape of history is replete with names of emperors and dictators who were viciously cruel, delighting in nothing more that causing Christians tremendous pain through torture. Many were impaled on wooden stakes and set ablaze as torches. Others were fed to lions or other wild beasts for entertainment. When persecution comes in any form, times are not often comforting. What is or should be *always* comforting is to know God in Christ and to know that He will not give us more than we can bear.

Think of William Tyndale, who was burned at the stake because he had the temerity to go against the Catholic Church and translate the Bible into the tongue of the masses. This would allow people to read the Bible for themselves, which is exactly what the Catholic Church did not want. Tyndale died for the crime of bringing God's Word to the common person.

2. *"It is not good news that God's plan has been thwarted in the past. It is not good news that God had to come up with an alternative plan since Israel rejected Christ."*

In addition, it would *not* be good news, if that were what actually occurred. God's plans have *never* been thwarted. The trouble with the Covenant position is that it sees absolutely no problem with the fact that God has supposedly completely *rejected* Israel (in spite of His many promises fully stating that He would *never* do that, a point which we have covered repeatedly). What then, are the implications of the Covenant position? It is the same as what they charge the Dispensationalist with: that God *changed* His mind. The fact that they believe God has simply *transferred* remaining blessings to the Church does not get around the problem of Covenant Theology labeling God a liar. If God could change His mind about Israel, could He not do the same with the Church? What would keep *that* from happening under the Covenant model? Nothing.

In effect then, the Covenant model is less comforting, because it teaches that God cast off Israel *completely* and *forever* and this is something that He could do to the Church. However, this is *not* what the Bible teaches. God's many promises to Israel are *forever* and He often swears by Himself because there is no one greater for Him to swear by in His unconditional covenants with Israel.

There *never* was a Plan B. What happened, happened because God *decreed* everything in eternity past. How is it *not* comforting to know that God has everything under complete and total control?

3. *"It's the way that too many dispensationalists teach the Second Coming of Christ. Their presentation is oriented toward fear for the Christian rather than faith."*

First, that is untrue. The Dispensational teaching of Christ's return should *not* induce fear in *any* Christian because the Rapture occurs *prior* to the Great Tribulation. If the Christian is no longer here on earth, how is it that Dispensationalism creates fear?

Figure 13, labeled *The Rapture and the Second Coming*, highlights the stark differences between these two events. To further highlight

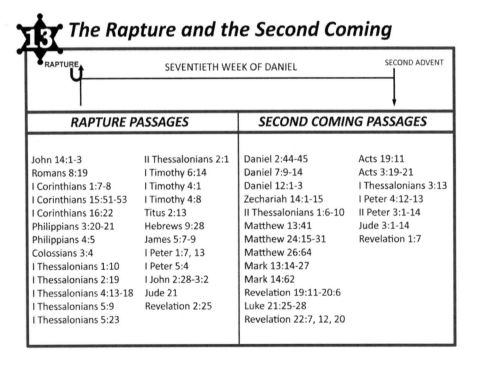

Comparing and Contrasting the I Thessalonians 4 and Matthew 24 Passages

I Thessalonians 4:13-18	Matthew 24:27-31
1) the Lord Himself will come down from heaven	1) all eyes will see Him coming
2) with a loud command	2) sun will be darkened
3) with the voice of an archangel	3) moon will not give its light
4) with the trumpet call of God	4) stars will fall from the sky
5) dead will rise first	5) heavenly bodies will be shaken
6) those who are alive will follow	6) sign of the Son of Man will appear in the sky
7) all caught up together	7) He will arrive on the clouds in the sky
8) will meet the Lord in the clouds	8) with power and great glory
9) will be with the Lord forever	9) He will send His angels with a loud trumpet
	10) angels will gather His elect
	11) from the four winds
	12) from one end of heaven to the other

the differences, look at **figure 14**, labeled, *Comparing and Contrasting...* I have used both of these charts before, and they are created based on information found in books by Renald Showers and Arnold G. Fruchtenbaum. The truth appears to be obvious. **Figure 15**, labeled, *"Premillennialism in the Old Testament"* highlights information culled from books by Renald Showers.

The only way to ignore the clear teachings of prophecy related to the End Times is to *allegorize* everything, which is unfortunately, what the Covenant Theologian does as the *norm* when dealing with these issues. In doing so, he arrives at the conclusion that nearly all prophecy has already been fulfilled, except maybe the last two chapters of Revelation. These last chapters show the end of the world as a wonderful victory over everything including death, hell, and Satan himself.

Certainly, that is the picture; however, it does not come without a massive tribulation, of which Christ spoke about in Matthew 24: the Olivet Discourse. Christ Himself said that there would be Tribulation such as the world had never seen. He even stated that if the days were not cut short no flesh would survive, but because of the elect

INTRODUCTORY NOTES:
- Premillennialists have often been criticized for basing their belief in a Millennium entirely on one passage of Scripture, Revelation 20.
- Because it is found in a book well noted for its high use of symbols, critics say it is foolish to take the one thousand years literally.
- While it is true that the Book of Revelation uses many symbols, the meaning of all those symbols is explained either within the book of Revelation itself or elsewhere in the Scriptures.
- Years are never used in a symbolic way in the book of Revelation (and if they are symbolic, the symbolism is nowhere explained).
- The mention of 1,260 days, 42 months, and 3½ years are all literal and not symbolic. There is no need to take the one thousand years as anything but literal years.
- The desire to spiritualize the text always places the burden of proof on the interpreter. Without objective proof it will always result in a subjective interpretation.

REGARDING THE MILLENNIUM:
- The belief in the Messianic Kingdom does not rest on Revelation 20 alone. The basis for the belief in the Messianic Kingdom is twofold:
  1) there are the unfulfilled promises of the Jewish covenants; promises that can only be fulfilled in a Messianic Kingdom.
  2) there are the unfulfilled prophecies of the Jewish prophets.
- Numerous prophecies of the Old Testament speak of the coming of the Messiah Who will reign on David's Throne, and rule over a peaceful Kingdom. There is a great amount of material in the Old Testament on the Messianic Kingdom, and the belief in a Messianic Kingdom rests on the basis of a literal interpretation of this massive material.

ABOUT THE MESSIANIC KINGDOM:
- There are two things about the Messianic Kingdom which were not revealed in the Old Testament, but revealed only in Revelation:
  1) the length of the Messianic Kingdom.
  2) the circumstances by which the Kingdom would come to an end, and how this would lead into the Eternal Order.

Premillennialism in the Old Testament

God's Eternal Covenants to Israel

Abrahamic Covenant (Gen 12:7; 13:15)	Land Covenant (Deut. 30:5; Joel 2:18-27; 3:18; Ezekiel 20:42-44; 34:25-31; Amos 9:13)	Davidic Covenant (II Samuel 7:11b-16; I Chronicles 17:10-15)	New Covenant (Jeremiah 31:31-34)	Isaiah 2:2-4	Isaiah 11:6-9
Promised Eternal Seed developing into a nation. Will possess the Promised Land with definite borders. For this promise to be fulfilled, there must be a future Kingdom.	Spoke of a worldwide regathering of the Jews and repossession of the Land following their dispersion.	Promised four eternal things: 1) an eternal house 2) an eternal throne 3) an eternal kingdom 4) one eternal Person	Covenant promises national regeneration and salvation of the nation of Israel encompassing each individual Jewish member of that nation.	The prophet speaks of universal peace in the world, which will only occur when Christ reigns from David's Throne. War will no longer exist and will be completely forgotten.	Universal peace will extend even to the animal kingdom. All animals will return to the Edenic state and become vegetarians. Man and snake, will be able to live in compatibility
Ezekiel 37:1-23		Jeremiah 33:17-26		Amos 9:11-12	Isaiah 14:12
Ezekiel is first commanded to prophesy over the dry bones scattered all over the valley (vv. 1-6). When he does, the bones all come together with sinews and skin, and then the breath of life is given to them so they become alive again (vv. 7-10). As God interprets the Vision of the Valley of Dry Bones (vv. 11-17), these bones are said to represent the whole House of Israel, which has become spiritually dead and dispersed (v. 11). Yet God will regather them, and they will again possess the Land (vv. 12-13).		Emphasis in this passage is on the eternality of and the impossibility of breaking the Davidic Covenant. The House of David will never become extinct (vv. 17-18). God is not through with Israel (vv. 23-24), but will fulfill every promise of the Davidic Covenant (vv. 25-26a) and the Abrahamic Covenant (v. 26b).		When the Kingdom is established, the ruins of the House of David will be repaired, and the Davidic Throne will again exercise all the glory of the days gone by (v. 11). This authority will extend to all the Gentile nations (v. 12). The promises that God made to Israel have not been rendered null and void, but will be fulfilled.	Israel will become the center of Gentile attention after their restoration. After Israel's regeneration and restoration (v. 1a), Gentiles will align themselves with Israel in order to worship the God of Israel (v. 1b). The Gentiles will be possessed by Israel and will become the servants of Israel (v. 2b).

the days will be cut short. That is not too comforting, is it? So, do we then call Jesus a liar, or do we simply decide that the fall of Jerusalem in A.D. 70 was the "End Times" and the Antichrist was the Roman Emperor *then*? On the other hand, maybe the Antichrist was Nero. Alternatively, maybe the Antichrist is the Roman Catholic Church. When Scripture is allegorized, interpretations can lead to any conclusion, and the interpreter then becomes the *subjective* determiner of what the text means. Showing conclusively how a particular interpretation is arrived at is not even a prerequisite.

It is common to hear Covenant Theologians say that there is nothing to fear because all except the last few chapters of Revelation have already occurred. What if they are wrong?

The fact that there is nothing to fear is a sentiment with which this author would agree. There *is* absolutely *nothing* for Christians to fear as we approach the end of the age. If what the Dispensationalist says is true (based on what the Bible teaches), why should the Christian fear anything? According to Dispensationalism, the Rapture will occur *before* the Tribulation. How is this not comforting?

Gillespie continues with, *"Granted, the truth that Jesus will return and judge the earth in righteousness ought to inspire fear and awe in sinners. It should drive them to their only hope -- Jesus Christ. But, in many circles this fear is urged as much upon believers as it is sinners. Instead of inspiring the believer to faith that Christ will return and complete his salvation, one is provoked to fear whether they might be ready when the Lord returns. I have heard many people, who were raised under this teaching, say that as a small child, they returned home (from*

school, etc.), found it unexpectedly empty, and then were struck with anxiety attacks, out of fear of being left behind. Is this the comfort the

Gospel gives? No! It is a message of apprehension and insecurity. I believe dispensational teaching contributes to this message."[68]

It can be assumed then that Gillespie is not aware of his own contradictions in this statement. On one hand, he is all for the Lord returning and says that it *should* inspire fear and awe, yet on the other hand he blames Dispensationalism for those who inordinately teach that fear is the underlying message of the Gospel. He has not even proven (by providing concrete examples) that it has been Dispensationalists who have endeavored to instill fear in Christians.

One needs only to look to the example of Charles Finney, a Presbyterian minister of the 1700s. Finney, who had a Calvinistic background, came to reject at least some of Calvin's teachings, preferring instead the role of an evangelist.[69]

Finney became known for his use of the "hellfire-and-brimstone" type of sermon to cause people to be afraid *not* to become Christians. His fear-inducing sermonizing was used to stir people emotionally into wanting to escape hell solely because it was hell. Often criticized for his lack of cogent and recognizable doctrine, he blistered onward in spite of the opposition and questions regarding his own conversion and qualification to be an evangelist.

There are other individuals as well, coming after Finney, who in some ways carried the torch forward. They used rational argumentation and emotionalism to engender fear within their congregants.

If anything, Dispensationalism presents a clear picture of the End Times, with the understanding that Christ comes to rescue His Bride prior to the Tribulation. This is a completely different event than the Second Coming, since at the Rapture He is *not* returning to earth. He rescues the remainder of faithful humanity, including faithful Jews, at

---

[68] http://www.inchristalone.org/ProblemsDispen.htm
[69] http://en.wikipedia.org/wiki/Charles_Finney

the end of the Great Tribulation. He then sets up His Millennial reign. After this, the Great White Throne, and then the Eternal Order begins. It is difficult to understand how any of this is not comforting for the Christian.

Gillespie finishes things off with this statement: "*This is well illustrated in the book and movie 'Left Behind.' The purpose, as given by Tim LaHaye, is to present a fictional representation of what might happen after the Rapture occurs. As with other such attempts... an element of **fear is created over what might happen to those who miss the Rapture***"[70] (emphasis added).

In responding to the bolded part of his last sentence, all that can be said is that *IF* the Rapture occurs, as the Dispensationalist believes it will, then those who have been left have *reason* to fear! They will have missed the boat, just as those living in Noah's day did, and we know that God's judgment literally rained down upon *them*, destroying all living things. However, in the case of any future Tribulation, they will *not* have missed all the chances to receive Christ as Savior, as the Holy Spirit will continue to work throughout the Great Tribulation. This is also comforting, because God will continue to make salvation available to those who were not taken in the Rapture. Again, how is this *not* comforting? God is making every possible opportunity available for salvation.

"Dispensationalism Is Not Comforting"
John the Baptist preached hell. Christ preached hell. Paul, James, and Peter talked about hell. It is the downside of *not* being saved and needs to be preached to those who are not *yet* saved. The authentic Christian has absolutely *nothing* to fear where hell is concerned. Nothing.

Salvation in Jesus Christ means two things:

---

[70] Ibid

1. We are saved *from* corruption, hell and eternal death
2. We are save *to* incorruption, heaven and eternal life

Anyone who preaches only *half* of that should not preach any of it. It is *necessary* for people to know that Christ wants to save them *from* something and nothing *they* can do will save themselves. They also need to know what He wants to save them *to* and that He is the only One who can accomplish it. This is the gospel message as presented by the New Testament.

When Christ returns at His future Second Coming, the Church will already be with Him. His pre-appointed task at that time will be the judgment of the nations (otherwise known as the Parable of the Sheep and the Goats).

The very *first* thing Jesus does upon His future physical return is to destroy the Antichrist with the breath of His mouth. Make no mistake; the Bible teaches that when He returns, the earth will have gone through unspeakable horrors. That is something to fear for those who will miss the Rapture. Frankly, I cannot imagine how absolutely terrifying it will be to live in those days. Once the Church is gone, the Holy Spirit, Who presently works *through* the Church to save people and restrain evil, will be moved out of the way. The influencing nature of the Holy Spirit will no longer be working *through* a body of believers. Literally, the gates of hell will be opened and beings from the darkness of that world will infiltrate this one. If you do not believe me, then please open your Bible to the book of Revelation and start reading.

If they are wrong, the Covenant Theologian is guilty of teaching anti-biblical theology. They will have robbed people of the truth they so desperately need to know; the truth that *does* comfort. They are telling everyone not to worry. It is all good. The fact of the matter is that people who are *not* Christians *should* worry. They need Jesus and it does not matter whether they are Jew or Gentile. They need Him. They need His truth and they need His salvation.

The Christian's salvation should also be his comfort. If his is living a life that bring dishonor to God, while his salvation is secure, he will certainly end up on the receiving end of God's chastising hand. For the true Christian, the thought of dying or being Raptured up to meet Him in the clouds does *not* bring fear. It brings rejoicing.

What comforts the Christian is knowing that the judgment of our sin took place at Calvary's cross. What comforts the Christian is the fact of our new life in Him. What comforts the Christian is knowing that when we see Him, we will be *like* Him. What comforts the Christian is knowing that in spite of *anything* they may suffer in this life, it will pale mightily in comparison with the full joy that awaits us when we see Him.

Dispensationalism approaches the Scripture as it is: God's Word to be taken literally (not *literalistically*). The constant misrepresentation of Dispensationalism is done based on an absolute inability to comprehend the simplest of theological and prophetic discourse.

Salvation has *never* been earned. Neither Adam nor Eve was required to earn it, and it is not earned now. God gave a gift through Jesus Christ His Son. It is all by grace and it is received by faith. That faith is *activated* when the Holy Spirit causes a spiritually blind person to *see*. Without the Spirit's work, no amount of trying will quicken the kind of faith that saves anyone. It is *all* God's work, from start to finish.

Chapter 9
Fra-Gee-Lay

It should be obvious to the impartial reader by now that Dispensationalism is not only *not* heretical, but indeed espouses *truth*. What is needed more than ever with Christians today is having and using *discernment*, a commodity that is severely lacking among Christians.

Covenant Theology seems to have missed the mark with their own system of interpretation where the Bible is concerned. They have also misrepresented Dispensationalism and then found it wanting. It is not unlike the evolutionist who views the world. He sees the same world that the Christian sees, but to the evolutionist, it is not God's Creation, but merely chance production.

Sadly, this is how Covenant Theologians see God's world and the Bible. They have the exact same information as the Dispensationalist, yet instead of seeing the entirety of God's *multi-faceted plan*, they see one thing and one thing only, which in itself becomes the end goal - *salvation*.

It is not unlike the father in "A Christmas Story," who after receiving a wooden crate containing his "major award," believes that the word stenciled across the top of the box is actually Italian, and pronounces it *fra-gee-lay*. Fortunately, his wife is right there to correct him and fortunately, he is humble enough to listen.

The Dispensationalist sees salvation as being *one* of the most important aspects of God's overall plan, in which *all things* do and will bring absolute glory and honor to God.

We have addressed many of the charges that have been leveled against Dispensationalism. Let us take a few moments to sum up the difficulties we have encountered:

1. **Misrepresentation:** This is one of the largest problems, which exists because another meaning is applied to what is written or stated by Dispensationalists. The example of their *own* meaning for the use of the word *plan* for instance, is a case in point. Since *Covenant Theology* equates *plan* with *salvation*, it is then assumed that this is what is meant when the Dispensationalist uses it. We have shown that God Himself uses the term *plan* as a *plurality* (not in the singular, as the Covenant Theologian does).
2. **Progressive:** We have shown that it is clear from Scripture that God's plan for *all* things was revealed to man in *stages*.

We believe we clearly indicated that this simply means that God chose to reveal *new* information to humanity, *not* as a condition of salvation, but to impart more information and responsibility. We have also pointed out that God has revealed His will on a *need to know* basis. The more He reveals to man, the more is revealed to Satan. One of the most important reasons He has chosen to reveal aspects of His multi-faceted plan to humanity in *stages* has to do with keeping Satan and his minions in the dark regarding those plans and purposes.

3. **Never Changing:** We have responded to the Covenant Theologian's charge that Dispensationalism allegedly teaches that salvation was largely of works for the Old Testament saint, and grace alone for the New Testament saint.
  In doing so, we believe we have also shown that it is actually Covenant Theology which espouses that salvation at one point in time was *merited* by the works of man (Adam and Eve). This is clearly *not* taught in Scripture, as salvation has *always* been and *remains* a work of God, received by faith.

4. **Failure:** We have addressed what we believe to be Covenant Theology's faulty notion that Dispensationalism advocates the failure of God. We have presented the truth that not only does the Dispensationalist *not* believe or endorse the perception that God has failed, but it is actually Covenant Theology which promotes this idea, regarding their view of Israel. The Dispensational teaching is that Israel did not utterly and permanently fail, but that God *blinded* them (as Paul clearly states in Romans 9-11) in order that He (God) might bypass Israel and work directly with Gentiles. Once the fullness of the Gentiles is established, *then* God will once again turn His attention back to Israel.

5. **God's Highest Purpose:** Throughout Scripture, it should be obvious that the highest purpose of God is *not* found in salvation. We believe that we have clearly established, that while

salvation is extremely important as a truly priceless gift of God, it is only one of the ways, which God chose to establish His highest purpose. That purpose is to bring glory to Himself by highlighting His absolute sovereignty over everything.

It has also been demonstrated that it is Covenant Theology, which is locked into the notion that salvation is God's highest purpose, which makes the Bible man-centered. In other words, Covenant Theology teaches that everything God has done, He has done for *man* whereas the Dispensationalist believes that everything He has done, He has done for His own *glory*.

6. **Inducing Fear:** While there are many rewards for the Christian, the Bible clearly establishes the fact that judgment is coming to those who are not in the Body of Christ, and to the earth itself. We have illustrated this by presenting the biblical End Times view of the Second Coming preceded by seven years of God's wrath (the Tribulation) as not only necessary, but also a legitimate way of preaching the full scope of the Good News, or Gospel of Christ.

   We have also shown that, far from inducing fear, the true understanding of the Rapture, the Tribulation and other events of the End Times, *does* promote comfort for the believer. Those in whom fear is induced need to question their own walk with the Lord and commitment to Him.

7. **Impugning God's Sovereignty:** We believe we have shown that God is fully and completely sovereign, relying on nothing apart from Himself to bring His plans, will, and purposes to fruition. We believe we have answered the false charge that the Dispensationalist impugns God's sovereignty. This – as has been shown – is the furthest thing from the actual. Dispensationalism goes beyond Covenant Theology in grasping

the true meaning of God's sovereignty. God is not dependent upon man in any way, shape, or form. Man is *fully* dependent upon Him. It is once again due to a misunderstanding of what Dispensationalism espouses, which has lead to a misrepresentation of the same.

In the final analysis, we believe it is Covenant Theology, which has erred and erred grievously. Covenant beliefs routinely deny that God has any plans for future Israel, in spite of God's promises to the contrary.

Dispensationalism is *not* the enemy of the cross. It is *not* the enemy of Christ. It is not a heretical teaching that supposedly espouses two methods of salvation.

Salvation is by grace, through faith, in Christ. Works was *never* part of the salvation equation. Never. It has always been *of* God *for* humanity, as a gift beyond measure. A gift is always unmerited; never earned. However, in the end, salvation, along with everything else God commits to accomplish, is done for the highest purpose possible: the recognition of His sovereignty.

Chapter 10
God's Unchallenged Sovereignty

Before ending this book, it is extremely important for the reader to understand God's sovereignty. Certainly, there is much we will never grasp about God's character and much that we will miss regarding His sovereignty. However, there are some basic truths concerning His sovereignty that should *not* be missed.

All of God's purposes *will* be accomplished. To support this, only a few Scripture passages need be noted. Let us start with Deuteronomy 32:39: *"See now that I, even I, am he, and there is no god beside me; I kill and I make alive; I wound and I heal; and there is none that can deliver out of my hand."*

Here are some others:

- Job 42:2: "*I know that you can do all things, and that no purpose of yours can be thwarted.*"
- Psalm 22:27-28: "*All the ends of the earth shall remember and turn to the LORD, and all the families of the nations shall worship before you. For kingship belongs to the LORD, and he rules over the nations.*"
- Proverbs 16:9: "*The heart of man plans his way, but the LORD establishes his steps.*"
- Proverbs 19:21 "*Many are the plans in the mind of a man, but it is the purpose of the LORD that will stand.*"

A favorite passage of mine is Psalm 2. It is worthwhile to note the entire passage here:

"*Why do the nations rage and the peoples plot in vain? The kings of the earth set themselves, and the rulers take counsel together, against the LORD and against his Anointed, saying, 'Let us burst their bonds apart and cast away their cords from us.' He who sits in the heavens laughs; the Lord holds them in derision. Then he will speak to them in his wrath, and terrify them in his fury, saying, 'As for me, I have set my King on Zion, my holy hill.' I will tell of the decree: The LORD said to me, 'You are my Son; today I have begotten you. Ask of me, and I will make the nations your heritage, and the ends of the earth your possession. You shall break them with a rod of iron and dash them in pieces like a potter's vessel.' Now therefore, O kings, be wise; be warned, O rulers of the earth. Serve the LORD with fear, and rejoice with trembling. Kiss the Son, lest he be angry, and you perish in the way, for his wrath is quickly kindled. Blessed are all who take refuge in him.*"

Taking the time consider all that is within that Psalm, it is clear that God brings about His will in all things. Though man may attempt to thwart God's purposes, it cannot be done. Even so, look how patient God is, when He states, "Kiss the Son, lest He be angry." There is patience dotted throughout the Psalm, in spite of the fact that God's warnings point to real judgment. God is not mocked. Though man may believe himself to be powerful and even invincible, God will show man just exactly how powerless and limited he actually is compared to the awesome power of Almighty God.

This leads us to an extremely important point. Because God is sovereign, and according to the passages quoted above, God *will* bring about His purposes, it stands to reason then that man has *two* choices. They are: 1) to voluntarily, *with* fear and humility, bow to God, submitting to Him all that you *possess*, and all that you *are* in order for His will to be accomplished in and through you, or 2) resist God, attempting to keep for yourself all that you possess, and all that you are, knowing that His will is still going to be accomplished through you.

I believe this is of supreme importance. God's will is going to be completed and we can be carried along by the scruff of our necks, kicking and screaming, all the while thinking that we are our own person. Or we can humbly submit to Him, so that we are lining ourselves up *with* His will.

All the people who choose hell as their final destination by ignoring God's redeeming grace, *still* do God's will, though they may think that they are doing their own. This was the case with Pharaoh, Nebuchadnezzar, and countless other individuals who believed that they lived their lives, doing what they wanted to do, accomplishing what they wanted to accomplish. This is actually the furthest thing from the truth.

Everyone who has ever lived, is now living, or will ever live, does what God wants him or her to do. This is not mere "puppetry," absolving man from any responsibility for his crimes and sin. This is God's sovereignty in action, fully in control of all aspects of His entire Creation. How could it *possibly* be otherwise if we are going to say that God is sovereign?

Each person has a choice, but the choice is *not* whether they will or will not do God's will. The choice is *how* will they do His will? Will it be done all the while believing that they control their own destiny, or will be done with hearts that are glad to give up their own lives in order that His will be done in and through them, *knowingly*?

No one is, in reality, their own god, even though they may come to believe it. God's purposes will not falter or fail. His sovereignty has always been on display, but the problem is that some simply do not *recognize* this truth.

This will all be made clear for each individual – whether spirit being, or human being. All will acknowledge that God is fully and absolutely sovereign, by Himself, and no one who has ever been (or will ever be) is a threat to His sovereignty.

Dispensationalism has no problem whatsoever with understanding that God is fully sovereign over *everything* which He created. This is the overriding truth of all that He accomplishes. His sovereignty is what Creation was made to *recognize* and *understand*. It is in *voluntarily* recognizing and understanding His sovereignty that glory is given to Him.

May we endeavor to glorify Him more and more every day while we live. May we seek His face, in order to understand the comprehensive quality of His sovereignty. May we glorify Him through our adoration of Him, *because* He is sovereign.

God reigns. He reigns supreme. He will always reign supreme. There is no other who deserves our love, our adoration, and our worship. He is God, *the* Sovereign Most High. Holy is His Name, and may He receive blessing and honor from all that we do, think and say.

"Thank you, Father, for Your sovereignty that has never been challenged and never will be challenged. Teach us more about Your sovereignty. We pray this in the Name of Jesus. Amen."

Resources for Your Library:

BOOKS:

- *The Basis of the Premillennial Faith*, by Charles C. Ryrie
- *Biblical Hermeneutics*, by Milton S. Terry
- *The Christian and Social Responsibility*, by Charles C. Ryrie
- *The Church in Prophecy*, by John F. Walvoord
- *Dictionary of Premillennial Theology*, Mal Couch, Editor
- *Dispensationalism Tomorrow & Beyond*, by C. Cone, Ed.
- *Exploring the Future*, by John Phillips
- *Footsteps of the Messiah*, by Arnold G. Fruchtenbaum
- *Future Israel (Why Christian Anti-Judaism Must Be Challenged)*, by E. Ray Clendenen, Ed.
- *Interpreting the Bible*, by A. Berkeley Mickelsen
- *Israelology*, by Arnold G. Fruchtenbaum
- *The Moody Handbook of Theology*, by Paul Enns
- *The Mountains of Israel*, by Norma Archbold
- *The Pre-Wrath Rapture Answered*, by Lee W. Brainard
- *Prolegomena*, by Christopher Cone
- *The Promises of God , a Bible Survey*, by Christopher Cone
- *There Really Is a Difference!* by Renald Showers
- *Things to Come*, by J. Dwight Pentecost
- *The Truth War*, by John MacArthur
- *What on Earth is God Doing?* By Renald Showers

INTERNET:

- Ariel Ministries — www.ariel.org
- Friends of Israel — www.foi.org
- Grace to You — www.gty.org
- Rightly Dividing — www.righly-dividing.com
- Study-Grow-Know — www.studygrowknow.com
- Tyndale Theological Seminary — www.tyndale.edu

NOTES

Made in the USA
Charleston, SC
19 January 2010